MEXICO

TITLES IN THE MODERN NATIONS OF THE WORLD SERIES INCLUDE:

Canada
China
Cuba
England
Germany
Italy
Mexico
Russia
Somalia
South Korea

MODERN
NATIONS
—OF THE—
WORLD

MEXICO

BY WILLIAM GOODWIN

LUCENT BOOKS
P.O. BOX 289011
SAN DIEGO, CA 92198-9011

*Dedicated to the friends who shared my early adventures in Mexico,
especially Louisa and Tecalote Blanco.*

Library of Congress Cataloging-in-Publication Data

Goodwin, William, 1943–
    Mexico / by William Goodwin.
       p.   cm. — (Modern nations of the world)
    Includes bibliographical references (p.   ¯) and index.
    Summary: Discusses the history, geography, climate, government,
culture, people, and modern aspects of Mexico.
    ISBN 1-56006-351-3 (lib. : alk. paper)
    1. Mexico—Juvenile literature. [1. Mexico.] I. Title.   II. Series.
F1208.5.G66 1999
972—dc21   98-29730
                                               CIP
                                               AC

Copyright © 1999 by Lucent Books, Inc.
P.O. Box 289011, San Diego, CA 92198-9011
Printed in the U.S.A.

CONTENTS

INTRODUCTION
MEXICO, A LAND OF CONTRASTS AND REVOLUTION

At government institutions, each day begins the same way in Mexico. As a band, or perhaps a lone bugle, plays, uniformed soldiers raise the nation's green, white, and red flag with the emblem of the eagle perching on a cactus and gripping a snake in its sharp beak. If the observer of this daily ritual should happen to be in the main square of the capital—in other words in the center of the world's largest city—the flag-raising ceremony will be particularly grand, but it will be hard to hear the band over the din of traffic.

On the roads encircling the plaza, the plaza built on the ruins of the ancient Aztec capital, thousands of the city's three million vehicles roar by, everything from bulletproof, chauffeur-driven limousines to smoke-belching jalopy-buses. Across the square well-groomed lawyers and businessmen in suits and ties rush in and out of the National Palace. Dark-skinned Indian peasants in soiled clothes worn on the bus ride from outlying villages squat along the sidewalk to sell their services or wares. In the distance two snow-capped volcanic peaks rise above the tall mountains ringing the city. As the morning progresses, however, the mountains disappear as smog rolls down from the northern edge of the mega-lopolis called Mexico City where more than one hundred thousand factories pollute the air.

In the main plaza of the capital and in cities and villages all over the country, it is the same: the ancient alongside the modern, wealth amidst poverty, organization next to chaos. Modern Mexico is defined by its historical, cultural, economic, and geographic contrasts. These contrasts are the result of a rich and complex cultural heritage in which Indian and European roots are tangled in centuries of epic and often violent struggles set in a vast geographic realm.

Mexico's original inhabitants were American Indians who had developed widespread urbanization, architectural design, irrigation technology, and intense agricultural productivity well before the birth of Christ. In 1517 the Spanish conquistadors invaded Mexico. Since then Mexico has been invaded by France, the United States (twice), and Spain (a second time). In the intervening centuries, numerous revolutions and civil wars tore through the country with great losses of lives, money, and national productivity. Since independence from Spain, a series of dictators has eliminated Mexican constitutions almost as fast as they were written.

But during all the violence and social turmoil, something wondrous happened. In the face of such adversity, the different peoples that came to live in Mexico succeeded in

Cars line up at a busy intersection in Mexico City. Some 3 million vehicles travel daily through the nation's capital, adding to the city's high pollution levels.

Native vendors make crafts and needlework to sell. These women, like many other Mexicans, share a rich Indian heritage.

blending their cultures and bloodlines to form a nation. And this nation reflects both its Indian and European heritage. The dual nature of Mexico's people is evident in their art, architecture, language, religion, music, and food.

Today Mexico is on a hopeful new path. With a true multiparty democracy functioning for the first time in many generations and with an economy fueled by one of the largest oil reserves of any country on Earth, Mexicans have the best opportunity for prosperity and social equality they have ever had in the country's long history.

The Geography and Climate of Mexico

With thirty-one states and one federal district covering about 756,000 square miles (1,958,000 square kilometers), the Republic of Mexico is the world's eighth largest country, and the third largest in Latin America after Brazil and Argentina. From its long northern border with the United States, 1,600 miles (2,576 kilometers) in length, to its southern borders with Guatemala and Belize, Mexico is positioned like a bridge between North America and Latin America. While Mexico's borders and its position in the center of the Americas have helped to shape the country's relationships with other nations, it is the nation's geography that has most profoundly affected the people living there.

Mexico has thousands of miles of coastline and long chains of tall mountains, arid deserts and tropical jungles, coral reefs and volcanic islands, rich farmland and evergreen forests. Such geographic diversity means that frigid, temperate, and searing climates can all occur in Mexico on the same day. It also means that some areas are ideally suited for human habitation while others are hostile to settlement.

A Land by the Sea

Mexico's lengthy coastlines total more than 6,000 miles (over 10,000 kilometers). In the entire Western Hemisphere only Canada has a longer coastline. Mexico's shores comprise coasts on the Gulf of Mexico, the Caribbean Sea, the Gulf of California, and the Pacific Ocean. Because of their nation's extensive contact with the sea, many Mexicans depend on fishing for their livelihood, and all over the country, even far inland, seafood is an important part of the Mexican diet. Furthermore, numerous deep-water ports allow Mexico to ship many oil products and a great variety of exports by sea.

Mexico also has numerous large islands. Some of the Pacific islands are true oceanic islands, geologically distinct from the mainland (Guadalupe and the Revilla Gigedo Archipelago).

Most of Mexico's islands, however, are close to shore and geologically linked to the mainland (for example, Cozumel in the Caribbean, Espiritu Santos in the Gulf of California, and Cedros in the Pacific). Many of these islands are inhabited, and a few, like Cozumel, are popular tourist destinations.

Major peninsulas extend from both the east and west coasts of Mexico. In the northwest part of the country is the isolated, extremely arid peninsula of Baja California. Beginning near the border with the United States, this peninsula runs southerly for nearly 800 miles (1,250 kilometers) with a width seldom more than 100 miles (160 kilometers). Consisting mostly of deserts and salt flats surrounding a rugged mountainous backbone, Baja California separates the Pacific Ocean from the Gulf of California (also called the Sea of Cortés). The Yucatán Peninsula extends into the Gulf of Mexico and the Caribbean Sea. Its flat limestone terrain is generally not higher than 500 feet (152 meters) above sea level. The islands of Cozumel and Islas Mujeres lie off the peninsula's northeast tip. The large, well-developed coral reefs that parallel the southern shores of the Yucatán attract undersea divers from all over the world.

Coastal Plains

Lowlands between the sea and the mountains dominate most of Mexico's coastal regions except for a few areas of high cliffs along the Pacific shoreline. On the east coast, the swampy Gulf Coastal Plain runs north and south for about 900 miles (1,450 kilometers), beginning at the border with Texas where it is 100 miles (160 kilometers) wide to the Yucatán peninsula where it terminates at the Tabasco Plain.

Mexico became an important producer of oil early in the twentieth century, but it was the huge oil deposits of the Gulf Coastal Plain that made the country a major player in the world oil market. By 1983 Mexico was already pumping a twentieth of the world's annual production of oil. Because of the oil deposits under the Gulf Coastal Plain, today Mexico is the fourth largest oil producer in the world and the fifth largest producer of natural gas.

The Pacific Coastal Plain is also about 900 miles (1,450 kilometers) long, but is much narrower and less well defined than the Gulf Coastal Plain. These lowlands begin near the Mexicali Valley at the border with California and extend to Tuxpan

in the south. Despite the name, the Pacific Coastal Plain faces the Gulf of California for more than half of its length. In the north, the Pacific Coastal Plain makes up part of the Sonoran Desert, which extends into California and Arizona. Though there is no oil under the Pacific Coastal Plain, a number of areas here prosper from large agricultural operations.

While most of Mexico's coastal plains are moderately populated with farming, ranching, and fishing communities, some large cities are also found here (for example, Veracruz on the east coast and Culiacán on the west).

An offshore drilling rig stands in the Gulf of Mexico. The Gulf Coastal Plain boasts large deposits of oil, making Mexico the world's fourth largest oil producer.

ISTHMUS OF TEHUANTEPEC

In the southern portion of the country, the seas seem to squeeze Mexico to form the narrow Isthmus of Tehuantepec. A low-lying (maximum altitude 900 feet/300 meters), windswept constriction of land, this isthmus lies between the waters of the Gulf of Campeche (on the Gulf of Mexico) to the north and the Gulf of Tehuantepec (on the Pacific Ocean) to the south. At its narrowest point, the isthmus is 137 miles (220 kilometers) wide, and it is only 120 miles (193 kilometers) between the Gulf of Campeche and the navigable waters of an inlet from the Gulf of Tehuantepec.

The Isthmus of Tehuantepec was once considered as the site for an interoceanic canal site. Panama was eventually chosen because intervening lakes in that nation lowered the total number of miles of canal that had to be dug. Instead of a canal across the isthmus, an American engineer named James Eads pushed for construction of a ship-carrying railway connecting the oceans. Even though this was considered by most people to be a more economical alternative to building the Panama Canal, his proposal was twice defeated by the U.S. Congress. In 1907 Mexico opened a regular railway line across the isthmus.

LAKES AND RIVERS

Many rivers and streams run to Mexico's coasts from the country's mountains and plateaus. Freshwater sources occur throughout the country except in the Yucatán and the most arid northwestern portions of the country. The country's largest natural body of fresh water is Lake Chapala (53 miles/ 86 kilometers long, 16 miles/25 kilometers wide) in the west-central state of Jalisco.

THE WINDS OF TEHUANTEPEC

The Isthmus of Tehuantepec is the only place in Mexico where the trade winds that blow unimpeded across the wide expanses of the Atlantic and the Caribbean are not blocked by mountains. As a result, from being a broad band out in the ocean, this wind is funneled into the relatively narrow space of the Isthmus of Tehuantepec. The trade winds tend to build up pressure for a few days until, all at once, the pressure is released. The result is two or three days of high winds that blast out into the Pacific with a force that even large ships try to avoid.

This wind (known locally as a Tehuantepecer) blows so much sand off the beach that a boat sailing too close to shore can have the paint sandblasted from its windward side. Boats traveling along the Pacific coast between the Panama Canal and North America have to decide between getting sandblasted while hugging the coast of the Gulf of Tehuantepec or going offshore where the winds generate huge waves. Most opt for the sandblasting.

Fresh water comprises one of Mexico's most vital natural resources. The many rivers flowing down from the Sierras and the *Altiplano* (high plain) pass through a system of dams that generate large quantities of hydroelectric power and fill over a third of Mexico's electricity requirements. Of the many rivers in Mexico, the largest is the Rio Bravo (known as the Rio Grande in the United States), which serves as the border between Mexico and Texas. Though both Mexico and the United States draw heavily from the Rio Bravo for irrigation, most of the water in the river actually comes from Mexican tributaries.

In many places mountains play an important role in shaping Mexico's rivers. Runoff from mountain rains and springs feeds the rivers, and mountain chains channel the flowing waters for great distances through the central plateau areas before allowing the rivers to run through valleys to the sea.

MOUNTAIN RANGES

Located on the volcanically active "ring of fire" that circles the Pacific Ocean, Mexico's topography is dominated by six major mountain chains. A story is told about how the sixteenth century conquistador Hernán Cortés described Mexico when he returned to Spain. The king asked him about the geography of Spain's new colony and Cortés, by way of reply, crumpled a sheet of paper and placed it on the table to show how ruggedly mountainous the area was.

Mexico is endowed with an abundance of precious metals and minerals important to industry, and the nation's mountains are where most of these resources are found. The mountains are riddled with mines that make Mexico the world leader in silver production, second in the production of graphite and bismuth, third in mercury, and fourth in arsenic and selenium. Other important mineral resources include sulfur, lead, zinc, coal, uranium, iron ore, gold, and copper. Minerals from Mexico's mountains account for the country's fourth largest source of income from exports (after oil, agricultural products, and machinery).

Mexico's numerous mountain ranges, called cordilleras, make up two-thirds of the landscape. These mountains not only shape much of the geography, but by blocking or channeling the weather coming in from the ocean, the cordilleras

THE RIO BRAVO

The Rio Bravo is the fifth longest river in North America. For more than half its length it forms the border between Texas and Mexico before flowing into the Gulf of Mexico. Most of the water in the Rio Bravo is supplied by its Mexican tributaries, the Salado, San Juan, and Conchos Rivers.

The Upper Rio Bravo Valley near Ciudad Juárez is the oldest irrigated region in Mexico. It was first cultivated by Pueblo Indians at least as long ago as A.D. 1200, more than three hundred years before the Spaniards arrived. Two major dams on the river provide water storage and prevent downriver flooding.

The Lower Rio Bravo Valley is home to some of the poorest and most decrepit towns in both the United States and Mexico. Corruption, drug smuggling, and pollution from chemical plants on the Mexican side, many of them owned by non-Mexican companies, make this region a dangerous place to live.

determine much of Mexico's climate. Because of their ruggedness, Mexico's mountainous areas tend to be remote, both in distance and in culture, from the main population centers. They are home to many of Mexico's Indians who farm small plots of land in the valleys and steep mountain sides.

The two longest cordilleras, running mostly north and south, make up the Sierra Madre (Spanish for Mother Range). The western branch of the Sierra Madre (Sierra Madre Occidental) is the geologic continuation of the North American Rockies and forms the longest cordillera. This rugged mountain chain consists mostly of volcanic rock covered with tropical vegetation at lower elevations and pine and oak forests near the peaks. A third of the country's large rivers begin in the mountains of the Sierra Madre Occidental. Running parallel to the Sierra Madre Occidental, the eastern branch of the Sierra Madre (Sierra Madre Oriental) consists mostly of softer limestone, and yet these eastern mountains are generally higher than the western Sierra Madre. Bathed all year long by the moisture-laden trade winds from the Gulf of Mexico, the eastern slopes of these mountains are covered with lush tropical foliage while the western slopes are arid.

The highest peak in Mexico, and the third highest in North America, is Pico de Orizaba (also called Citlaltépetl). Rising from one of the several cordilleras that link the two main branches of the Sierra Madre, this dormant volcano (last eruption in 1657) rises to a spectacular height of 18,700 feet (5,700 meters). Pico de Orizaba exemplifies the volcanic forces that built much of the central and southern part of the country. The country's volcanoes are exceptionally young in geologic terms. In fact, in 1943 a brand new volcano named Paricutín appeared where a cornfield had been.

The Southern Highlands are a series of mountain ranges and plateaus that run from the west-central part of the country near Puerto Vallarta southeast to the Isthmus of Tehuantepec. Collectively, these tall mountains are known as the Sierra Madre del Sur. In many places they arise steeply from the Pacific coastline to create spectacular backdrops to the string of sea ports and tropical tourist destinations known as the Mexican Riviera.

The Chiapas Highlands, south of the Isthmus of Tehuantepec, are an extension of the Central American mountains. The northwest part of these mountains is sliced by a rift valley where the large Grijalva River runs parallel to the coast before emptying into the Gulf of Mexico. The Chiapas Highlands, home to Mexico's poorest Indians, have long been neglected by the government in Mexico City. As a result, the remote villages of the area have spawned Mexico's newest revolutionaries who are able to use the rugged mountains as staging areas for raids on government forces.

Though the ruggedness of the cordilleras makes life there difficult, Mexico's great mountains are the framework for the plateaus, plains, and basins that make up the remainder of the nation's geography.

An aerial view of Copper Canyon, part of the rugged Sierra Madre mountain chain.

PLATEAUS

The vast Central Plateau, also known as the *Altiplano* (high plain), lies between the sparsely settled western and eastern cordilleras of the Sierra Madre. This plain covers about 40 percent of the country and makes up the third largest inhabited plateau in the world (after those in Tibet and Bolivia). The Central Plateau

EARTHQUAKES AND VOLCANOES

Geography sometimes has extremely unpleasant consequences in Mexico. In September of 1985, Mexico City was hit by the latest and worst of several twentieth-century earthquakes. This huge quake resulted in over seven thousand casualties and extremely heavy destruction in the central area of the city. The catastrophic destructiveness of the earthquake was blamed on the fact that most of Mexico City is built on the soft subsoil that has been used for centuries to fill in the many lakes that previously surrounded the growing capital.

Only fifty miles from Mexico City, the volcano Popocatépetl ("smoking mountain" in the Aztec language) rises to an altitude of almost 18,000 feet (5,400 meters). This volcano has not undergone a full eruption since 1702. Until it awoke in 1997, the only time in the twentieth century that "Popo" was active was in 1920. Then in May of 1997, "Popo" gave off a thunderous explosion followed by a stream of ash, rocks, and sulfur dioxide gas that shot two miles into the sky. With this increased activity, some scientists think Popo may be building up to a full eruption, and they have placed the entire region on yellow alert.

Volcanic activity in Mexico is not limited to Popocatépetl. In the twentieth century Mexico has experienced several eruptions from other volcanoes, both new and ancient. In 1943 the country's newest volcano emerged from a cornfield in the central state of Michoacán. Named Paricutín, it grew to 9,210 feet (2,800 meters) in height and destroyed several villages before becoming dormant in 1952. In 1982 a dormant volcano in the southern state of Chiapas roared back to life, erupting violently and killing many people.

A cloud of smoke and ash rises from Popocatépetl during its partial eruption on May 17, 1997. Scientists fear that "Popo" may stage a full eruption in the near future.

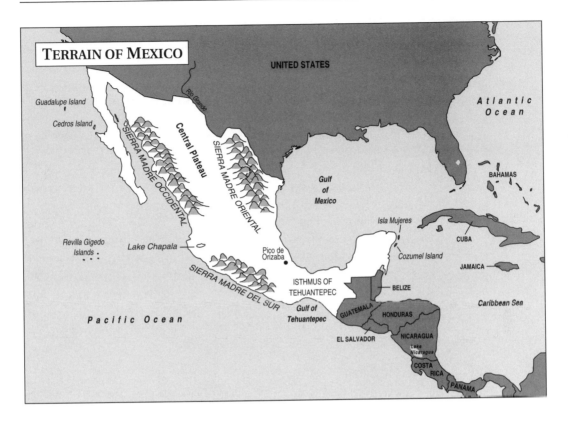

TERRAIN OF MEXICO

tilts upward, beginning at about 3,000 feet (1,000 meters) in the north and rising to about 8,000 feet (2,660 meters) south of Mexico City. Arid in the north, the fertility of this great plateau gradually increases as it progresses south where the land is heavily farmed.

A second important plateau runs east from the Guadalajara region to join the Central Plateau. This region is drained by the large Balsas River that flows into the Pacific at the Sea Port of Lázaro Cárdenas. Though it accounts for only about one-seventh of the country's land area, approximately half of Mexico's population lives here.

Although other parts of the country have volcanic soils that support excellent farming operations where irrigation is possible, the richest soils and best farming in all of Mexico are found in these central plateaus. Beginning long before the Spanish conquest, the promise of abundant food supplies from these fertile areas of the central plateaus has attracted people from less productive areas. Now these two plateaus are home to a majority of Mexico's citizens.

About 70 percent of Mexicans now live in urban centers, and most of those are in the two central plateaus. The major concentration of urban centers stretches as a narrow band across Mexico's central plateaus from Puebla to Guadalajara.

Mexico City is the nation's undisputed primary city. With a population of over twenty million, it is the political, economic, social, educational, and industrial capital of Mexico. Guadalajara is the country's second largest city. It is the regional capital of Jalisco and much of the western part of the country, and is an important educational, industrial, and cultural center. While the largest urban centers in Mexico (both on the plateaus and along the Mexico–United States border) are growing most rapidly, the populations of small and intermediate-sized cities are also increasing at a high rate.

Another plateau makes up most of the Yucatán Peninsula, the flattest and lowest land in the country. The Yucatán Plateau, consisting of limestone riddled with sinkholes called cenotes, is covered with tropical savannah and forest. The only significant population center of the Yucatán is Mérida.

DESERTS

Deserts, defined as arid regions receiving less than 10 inches (25 centimeters) of rain each year, comprise almost half of Mexico's land area north of the Isthmus of Tehuantepec. The areas are divided into two separate deserts, the Sonoran in the northwest and the Chihuahuan in the north-central part of the country. Both of these deserts also extend into the southwestern regions of the United States. Although much of Mexico's desert regions are sparsely inhabited, in areas where industry has grown or farming is possible due to irrigation, sizeable populations are found.

CLIMATE

A variety of climactic conditions occur in Mexico due to the country's geographical diversity. Even though much of the country lies within the tropical latitudes, the altitude of the mountains and the Central Plateau prevent it from being uniformly hot.

Northern Mexico lies within one of the world's great desert regions. These areas have minimum precipitation and wide extremes of temperature between winter and summer. In the Sonoran Desert, for example, the difference between the highest temperatures and the lowest is extreme. In July and August on the central Baja Peninsula, 110° F (45° C) is common while in the middle of winter the same area can reach 32° F (0° C).

More than half of Mexico lies south of the Tropic of Cancer. In most of these tropical regions, warm, moisture-laden air masses from the sea provide immense precipitation. Most of the rain in the tropical regions falls during the wet season (May through August). Destructive hurricanes are a danger on both tropical coasts from August through October. Within the Mexican tropics, temperatures vary less from season to season than in the desert regions. Often there is only about ten degrees difference in the upper and lower extremes from winter to summer.

In the tropics, the temperature range depends more on elevation than latitude. From sea level to 3,000 feet (912 meters) is the hot zone. For example, the average temperature at Veracruz on the Gulf Coast is 77° F (25° C). From 3,000 to 6,000 feet (912 to 1,824 meters) is the temperate zone. The average temperature at Jalapa, a town located at 4,600 feet

Cactuses are silhouetted against a cloudy sky in Mexico's Sonoran Desert.

(1,318 meters), is 66° F (19° C). From 6,000 to 11,000 feet (1,824 to 3,344 meters) is the cold zone, even in the tropics. The average temperature at Pachuca, a village located 8,000 feet (2,432 meters) high, is 59° F (15° C). Alpine meadows are found on the highest volcanic mountains, and above 13,000 feet (3,952 meters) there is a permanent snowline in Mexico's tropical latitudes.

Most of Mexico lacks adequate precipitation during at least part of the year. With the exception of some highland areas, all of Mexico north of the Tropic of Cancer receives less than twenty inches of rain per year. Baja California, Sonora, and Chihuahua receive less than ten inches per year. Central and southern Mexico receive less than forty inches per year. Only the Gulf Coastal Plain from Tampico south, the Chiapas Highlands near the Guatemalan border, and the southern part of the Yucatán Peninsula receive abundant year-round rainfall.

FLORA AND FAUNA

The immense differences in climate that occur within Mexico have given rise to an enormous variety of plant and animal life in Mexico. The diversity of plant life ranges from distinctive desert ecosystems to lush tropical rain forests.

The desert regions are home to plants adapted to arid conditions. These include many species of cactus, agave, mesquite, cassava, and the bizarre boojum tree of Baja California. The southern highlands and other mountainous areas are home to coniferous forests. In the high precipitation areas, particularly on the tropical coastal plains and the eastern slopes of the Sierra Madre Oriental, tropical vegetation predominates. Several of these areas, especially in the far south of the country, have dense stands of broadleaf evergreen trees of varying heights that form some of the most luxuriant and diversified rain forests in the world. The western coastal areas are covered with deciduous and semi-deciduous forests which lack the variety and density of tropical rain forests.

The poinsettia, a popular decorative plant often associated with Christmas, is native to Mexico. It grows wild in areas of high precipitation.

Because of Mexico's location astride the boundary dividing North and middle American fauna, a great diversity of animals are native to the country. Jaguars, tapirs, monkeys,

THE GRAY WHALES OF BAJA

The sea life off Mexico's coasts includes much more than kelp beds, coral reefs, seals, and fish. Among the abundant marine organisms found in Mexican waters are a variety of whales. Humpback, fin, sei, Bryde's, blue, sperm, and gray whales are residents or seasonal visitors in Mexican waters.

Each year the gray whales undertake the longest migration of any mammal on Earth. At the beginning of winter, these huge animals leave the cold North Pacific and migrate south. Swimming night and day, they travel approximately five thousand miles (8,065 kilometers) until at last they reach the lagoons and bays along the coast of Baja California. In the protected waters of the Baja California lagoons the whales mate and give birth to their calves.

Among these whales' many amazing feats, none has puzzled scientists as much as their feeding pattern. As far as biologists have been able to determine, the adult gray whales do not eat during the entire seven-to-eight-month migration.

Growing to over forty feet (12.2 meters) long and up to forty tons (36.3 metric tons), these whales were once hunted nearly to extinction. By the early twentieth century, gray whales had been hunted to extinction on the Atlantic coast, and less than three hundred remained of the eastern Pacific gray whale population. Thinking it might already be too late, international and U.S. agreements finally halted all hunting of these animals in 1972. Since then, the gray whale has made an astounding recovery: Now over 21,000 individuals make the annual migration from Alaska to Mexico.

A gray whale in Baja California's San Ignacio Lagoon spy hops, or pokes its head out of the water. During the winter months, gray whales migrate to the warm waters of Mexico.

The lush rain forests of Chiapas are home to a variety of tropical plant and animal species.

parrots, and anteaters in the south contrast with deer, pumas, coyotes, rabbits, snakes (at least a dozen species of rattlesnakes), and armadillos in the north. Unfortunately, thousands of years of constant human habitation have brought about conditions that have destroyed most of the natural habitat. Many species that once inhabited the Central Plateau and the Southern Highlands are no longer found there.

Ocean life off the coasts of Mexico is also extremely varied and abundant, the result, once again, of a variety of conditions. For example, six species of sea turtles and almost forty species of sea birds occur in Mexican waters. Biological diversity in the sea off Mexico is supported by the cool currents of the Pacific Ocean, the protected expanse of the Gulf of California, the turbid waters of the Gulf of Mexico, and the clear, warm Caribbean Sea.

From Prehistory to the Spanish Conquest

The very first people to inhabit what is today known as Mexico were small groups of nomads who had crossed the Bering Strait from their Asian homelands. They were hunters of game animals like mastodons, mammoths, bison, and antelope, and they were fishermen and gatherers of wild fruits and berries. Some anthropologists believe the first of these nomads arrived in Mexico as early as 24,000–40,000 years ago, but the oldest remains found so far (in the Valley of Mexico at Santa Isabel Ixtapan) date to about 9000 B.C.

At some point in Mexico's prehistory, an event occurred that would cause some of the nomads to form the first settlements in Mexico: they discovered the wild grass called maize, the ancestor of corn. At first these early inhabitants of the New World simply gathered the wild maize, but archaeological evidence indicates that around 5000 B.C. they began to cultivate it. Soon they discovered how to improve wild maize (which had only a single small spear of edible grain on each stalk) into a plant that produced many full ears of corn. Eventually the people of these early settlements also began cultivating other fruits and vegetables native to the New World, including avocadoes, chilies, beans, peanuts, tomatoes, potatoes, guavas, papayas, pineapples, and squashes.

The need to tend the crops made a year-round permanent settlement necessary, and as agriculture took root in Mexico, the previously nomadic people established the beginnings of what were to become great civilizations. By 2000 B.C. permanent farming settlements were well established in Mexico. These gave rise to the activities associated with advancing civilizations, including tool and pottery making, building permanent structures, and establishing systems of government.

Between the appearance of these earliest settlements and the arrival of the Spaniards (a period of at least thirty-five hundred years), a number of increasingly organized and advanced civilizations developed and flourished in Mexico. For ease of study, anthropologists divide this large and complicated historical period into three parts: preclassic, classic, and postclassic.

PRECLASSIC CIVILIZATIONS

Long before the birth of Christ, the central and southern regions of Mexico were inhabited by peoples thought to be descendants of the early nomads. As agriculture became more sophisticated, cultivation and hybridization techniques improved. With agriculture assuring an abundant supply of food, societies were able to expand their interests and develop. As a result, during the preclassic period (1200 B.C. to A.D. 250) settlements became more complex and political-religious centers appeared. The first of these to leave a prominent historical record was the civilization of the Olmecs.

Although the archaeological records are not complete, the Olmecs probably arose as early as 2000 B.C. Experts disagree about where they first appeared. The traditional view locates their earliest centers in the southern coastal plains (where the states of Veracruz and Tabasco are located today) because there are so many Olmec ruins there. More recently, however, other experts claim that Olmec remains found on Mexico's Pacific coast are older and therefore indicate that area as the original homeland. One day the mystery of where the Olmecs began their civilization may be solved, but this disagreement between experts emphasizes the difficulty in learning the truth about a people who lived so long ago.

It is known that from their centers in southern Mexico, the Olmecs expanded until their influence reached Guatemala and El Salvador to the south and the Valley of Mexico to the west. By 1000 B.C. the Olmecs were placing large stone sculptures in important sites. These carvings, usually made of volcanic basalt rock, are the most enduring legacy of the Olmecs. Some of them portray monumental heads, the tallest more than ten feet high, wearing headgear that looks similar to modern football helmets. The faces of these heads have thick lips, flat noses, and wide, staring eyes.

Besides advances in sculpture and pottery, the Olmecs invented a system of numbering, an amazingly accurate calendar, hieroglyphic writing, and a means of astronomical observation. They also invented a ceremonial court game us-

Measuring nearly ten feet tall, this sculpture marked an important site for the ancient Olmecs, a civilization that thrived in Mexico between 2000 and 400 B.C.

ing a rubber ball that is still played by Indians in some parts of southern Mexico. Though their architecture was not of the same grand scale as the later civilizations of the Teotihuacanos, Maya, and Aztecs, the Olmecs are believed to be the first people in the New World to build religious centers and pyramids.

The Olmecs hold a special place in the flow of cultures that rose and fell in the New World before the arrival of the Spaniards. As Europe was experiencing the Trojan War and the Golden Age of Athens, the Olmec civilization was laying the foundations of art, politics, religion, and economics that have inspired some anthropologists to call it the "mother culture" for the Indian civilizations that followed.

As the Olmecs were reaching their highest level of achievement, the Zapotecs and the Mixtecs of the Valley of Oaxaca in the southwestern part of Mexico began building ceremonial centers. The best example of their architecture is the spectacular Monte Alban where the Zapotec builders literally cut the top off a mountain to create a plateau for their city. At its peak, Monte Alban was home to about forty thousand Zapotecs.

Around 400 B.C., the Olmec civilization disappeared forever, apparently overrun by warriors from other areas. Eventually the Zapotec and Mixtec religious and cultural centers were also abandoned, but unlike the Olmecs who seemed to have either disappeared or been absorbed into other Indian groups, the Zapotecs and Mixtecs live in Oaxaca to this day. They continue to maintain a strong attachment to the ancient culture from which they sprang.

Near the end of the preclassic period, the first large urban centers appeared in Mexico, complete with monumental architecture and densely settled city life. One of the earliest of these cities was Teotihuacán in the Valley of Mexico which appeared about 150 B.C. The identity and origin of the builders of this great city were a mystery even to the Aztecs who simply called the ruins of Teotihuacán the abode of the gods. At its peak, this enormous city, more than eight square miles in area, was a busy cultural and economic center. Teotihuacán flourished for seven centuries, from the late preclassic period to the middle of the classic period. Around A.D. 650 it began a gradual decline until it was abandoned for unknown reasons about A.D. 750.

THE CLASSIC PERIOD

The classic period, hazily defined as the era when the large city-states appeared and grew to dominate the region, began about A.D. 250. Though Teotihuacán began its rise in the preclassic era, its peak coincided with the first half of the classic period. The most dominant culture of Mexico's classic period, however, is without a doubt that of the Maya.

Although scholars can trace the Maya back to approximately 50 B.C., the peak of their power stretched from A.D. 292 to A.D. 909, when their civilization extended throughout the Mexican states of Chiapas, Tabasco, Campeche, Yucatán, and Quintana Roo, as well as portions of Guatemala, Belize, and Honduras.

The influence of the Teotihuacán culture on the Maya is apparent in some of the Mayan clothing, art, religious symbols, and, especially, the building of tall stepped pyramids. By A.D. 500, pyramids rose from many Mayan city-states. The largest of these were at Palenque, Tikal, Copán, Quiriga, Altun Ha, Uaxactun, Calakmul, Yaxchilán, Tonina, and Comalcalco.

The Maya took mathematics to heights unequaled in Europe for several more centuries, and not until the twentieth century was there a calendar anywhere on Earth more accurate than the Mayan calendar of the fifth century.

By the height of their civilization in about A.D. 800, the Maya had also achieved great developments in astronomy,

THE MYSTERY AND GLORY OF TEOTIHUACÁN

Teotihuacán arose before the beginning of the Christian era to become the greatest metropolis in the Americas until the rise of the Aztec empire. At the height of its prosperity, about A.D. 500, Teotihuacán was as large as London would become a millennium later. Pyramids on the scale of the great Egyptian pyramids dominated the city's center.

With their capital dominated by the huge pyramids of the Sun and Moon and many hundreds of other large, multilevel structures, Teotihuacanos clearly excelled in architecture. They were also skilled painters, potters, and sculptors. The pyramids are surrounded by a vast city with the remains of wide streets, palaces, pottery and stone-working shops, administrative centers, sports fields, religious sites, and apartment-like complexes where most of the two hundred thousand people lived.

The communal homes of Teotihuacán possessed inner patios, altars, sewers, and drainage systems to prevent flooding during the rainy season. Chemical analysis of the kitchen areas has shown the diet of Teotihuacanos included corn, beans, squash, chili peppers, cacti, cherries, rabbits, deer, dogs, turkeys, ducks, and fish.

Writing in the December 1995 issue of *National Geographic* magazine, University of California archaeologist Karl Taube states, "We still don't know what language the Teotihuacanos spoke, where they came from, or what happened to them." Imperial Rome and Teotihuacán flourished at the same time in history, yet Teotihuacán, in a more harsh and arid environment, outlived Caesar's Rome. It is, therefore, surprising that after seven centuries of glory, so much of Teotihuacán remains a mystery. Their civilization so completely disappeared that even the Aztecs referred to the ruins of Teotihuacán simply as the Place of the Gods.

The Pyramid of the Sun rises amid the restored structures of the ancient capital of Teotihuacán.

writing, history, religion, and art. Mayan sculpture and architecture are considered some the most beautiful and dignified ever created.

Human sacrifice and the use of human blood in religious ceremonies were a part of most, if not all, early New World cultures, and the Maya were no exception. In addition to sacrificing enemy captives to the Mayan gods, Maya drew blood from their own bodies to appease their gods.

Many of the details of Mayan life and culture known to modern scholars come from a book written in the 1500s by Mayan converts to Christianity. The book, titled *Popol Vuh* (Book of the People), preserves historical and religious texts that had been passed down through Mayan hieroglyphics or by word-of-mouth in Quiche, an Indian language of that time. The missionaries did not know how to read the hieroglyphics, but they had learned Quiche and were therefore able to translate the *Popol Vuh* into Spanish.

By the time of the fall of Teotihuacán, the population of Mexico had grown to forty times its preclassic size. No single city-state could any longer serve as a unifying force for the entire region, and cultures throughout the area were almost

A reclining statue sits near the huge El Castillo pyramid in Chichén Itzá, which was once part of the vast Toltec empire.

constantly at war. Scholars guess that war combined with famine and disease led to the fall of both Teotihuacán and, two centuries later, the Mayan civilization.

The Postclassic Period

From the end of the classic period (about A.D. 900) until the Spanish arrived, war was a defining feature of the region's cultures. Fighting engulfed the south and central parts of Mexico as priest-rulers were replaced by military kings and the different groups became immersed in a bloody struggle for overall control.

The first warrior-based people to attain military success were the Toltecs who came to Central Mexico from the north. Between A.D. 900 and 1200, the Toltecs built a fortified capital at Tula (in present-day Hidalgo) and other centers that extended north to Zacatecas, south to Guatemala, and east to the immense pyramids of Chichén Itzá. Some speculate that it was the Toltecs who destroyed the Teotihuacán culture.

The chief rivals to the Toltecs were the Zapotecs and Mixtecs of Oaxaca, the Tarascans of Michoacán, and the Huastecs of northeastern Mexico. None of these groups consistently overpowered the others, so they coexisted in an uneasy truce. This all changed with the arrival, a little after A.D. 1200, of the Aztecs, the fiercest warriors Mexico has ever known.

According to the Aztec chronicles, their god of war led them south from their original home on a mysterious island in the north named Aztatlán, and then gave them a new name, *Mejica*. A prophecy stated that where they saw an eagle perched on a cactus holding a snake in its beak, they would build their new capital. Whether legend or history, this story is the origin of the national emblem that appears in the center of the Mexican flag and seal.

The place where the migrating Aztecs saw the prophesied eagle on a cactus was near present-day Mexico City. At this swampy location in 1325 the Aztecs began construction of their new capital. They named it Tenochtitlán.

When the Aztecs first arrived on the Central Plateau, they were hardly more than savages, but they learned fast from their more developed neighbors. Not only did they quickly adopt the agriculture and building methods of these other groups, they began improving them. They also embarked on a ruthless plan to rule their neighbors.

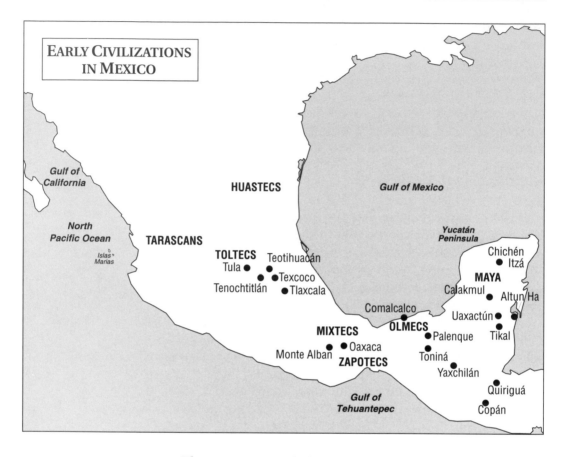

EARLY CIVILIZATIONS
IN MEXICO

Gulf of
California

North
Pacific Ocean

Islas
Marias

HUASTECS

Gulf of Mexico

TARASCANS

Yucatán
Peninsula

TOLTECS   Teotihuacán
Tula ●

●Texcoco
Tenochtitlán   ●Tlaxcala

Comalcalco ●

Chichén
● Itzá

MAYA
Calakmul
●   Altun Ha

Uaxactún ●
●

MIXTECS   OLMECS
●Oaxaca   ●Palenque   Tikal
Monte Alban ●   ●
ZAPOTECS   Toniná

Yaxchilán ●

Quiriguá
●

Gulf of
Tehuantepec

Copán

The Aztecs joined the nearby Tepanec kingdom, first as
mercenary warriors, then allies, and by 1375, as joint rulers
of the region. In 1428, under the fourth Aztec king, the Aztecs
overthrew the Tepanec and took over control of the Valley of
Mexico, the fertile region around Tenochtitlán.

Through brutal military domination, by 1500 Aztecs controlled all the lands and people of Central Mexico. By successfully invading the prosperous Toltec and Mayan centers,
the Aztecs caused a cultural collapse that has been compared with the fall of the Roman empire.

Aztec warriors were trained to believe they were destined
to die in battle and that when they died they would become
hummingbirds and fly to the sun. Not only were they fierce
fighters, the Aztecs practiced human sacrifice and ritual can-
nibalism upon their captives. Conquered by such brutal warriors, the other people of Mexico obeyed the Aztecs not out
of loyalty but out of fear. These conquered people were

forced to pay Tenochtitlán tribute and taxes in the form of precious stones and metals, feathers, foods, and other valuable commodities.

When the Spaniards arrived, the Aztecs were the dominant force in middle America and the Aztec language, Nahuatl, was a well-established language from Panama to western North America. Nahuatl is still spoken by Indians in several parts of Mexico.

THE SPANIARDS ARRIVE

After seventy years of war with the Moors, Spain had emerged as the most powerful nation in Europe in the fifteenth century. Believing that Spain's Roman Catholic god was destined to rule the world, the Spanish sent Christopher Columbus in search of new trade routes to India and the rest of the Far East. Columbus landed in the Caribbean in 1492 and soon after, the Catholic Pope gave the Spanish complete rights to any lands in the New World as long as the Spanish made "God's name known there." Soon the Spanish had established a colony on the island of Cuba.

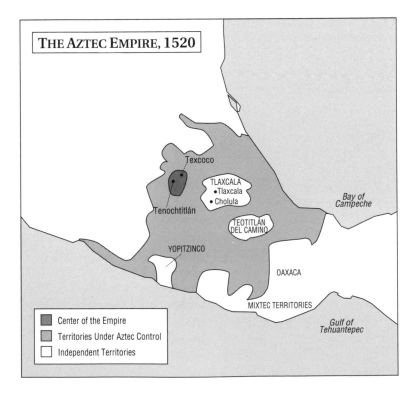

THE AZTEC CENTURY

In little more than a century the Aztecs, using shrewd alliances and treachery, extended their domination to an area covering most of present-day Mexico. This phenomenal success is largely explained by three factors: religion, economy, and organization.

The Aztec religion, dominated by the god of sun and war, Huitzilopochtli, urged warriors to acts of extreme bravery. Furthermore, Huitzilopochtli was believed to do battle with the moon and stars every day, and for this the top god needed strength. The only food acceptable to him was human blood. Therefore the Aztec religion called for human sacrifice, and it was mostly prisoners of war who were sacrificed. With such a fate awaiting anyone who fought and lost to the fierce Aztec warriors, enemies were much less willing to fight.

Besides an abiding interest in warfare, the Aztecs were an agricultural people. Gods of water, vegetation, and fertility were numerous and vital to their religious life. Religion was therefore the driving force behind studying the planets and stars, carving idols, building great temples, and developing an accurate calendar. But it is doubtful that religion alone could have produced such an advanced civilization.

The Aztecs also possessed a solid economy. Based on a highly productive agricultural system watered by a complex of irrigation canals, a large population, and a taxation/tribute system imposed upon subjugated neighbors, the Aztec homeland in the Valley of Mexico was able to amass wealth.

Outside the valley moving trade goods from one area to another was slow and inefficient since wheels were one thing these cultures had not invented. In the Valley of Mexico, however, the Aztecs built a system of efficient transportation that used boats to take advantage of the many lakes in the region. As a result, the Aztec capital had an abundance of food and other goods, a well-supplied military, and a wealthy merchant class.

Money in the form of coins and bills did not exist in preconquest Mexico. Certain items, however, were used much like money. These included sacks of cacao beans, quills from bird feathers that were filled with gold dust, and small copper axes. To make their economy work on such a large scale, the Aztecs had to devise an efficient system of social organization.

From the absolute rule of the king down to the lowliest worker, Aztec society was thoroughly organized into castes and classes. This social and political organization reached its peak under the ninth Aztec king, Montezuma II (also spelled Moctezuma), who ruled from 1502 to 1520. He oversaw a huge political, military, and religious organization with governors, tax collectors, courts, military prisons, schools for boys and girls, and mail services. All of the land was owned by the entire community, and only the most industrious farmers were assigned land to cultivate. The rulers, nobles, and wealthy merchants lived in fine homes while commoners lived in large apartment-like units housing the members of extended families.

Then, with the mighty Aztec civilization still growing, the Spaniards arrived.

Diego Velázquez, governor of Cuba, laid the foundation for the conquest of Mexico. In 1517 and 1518 he sent Francisco Hernández de Cordoba and Juan de Grijalva to explore the coasts of Yucatán and the Gulf of Mexico. When they returned with promising reports of a large population and great wealth on the mainland, Velázquez sent Hernán (also Fernando or Hernando according to various authors) Cortés to investigate.

The wisest and most humane of the Aztec gods was Quetzalcoatl who was frequently depicted with a beard. According to legend, Quetzalcoatl had been forced out of Mexico by another god, but he promised to return in the year *Ce Acatl* of the Aztec calendar (A.D. 1519). Then, during the year of *Ce Acatl*, an exhausted runner arrived in Tenochtitlán. He told Montezuma of strange beings with light skin and facial hair who had appeared from the sea on the eastern shore. For ten years prior to *Ce Acatl*, evil omens had been puzzling and worrying the Aztec king and his priests. Now with the arrival of the bearded strangers, the explanation for the omens seemed clear: Quetzalcoatl and his court had returned.

Cortés had left Cuba with eleven small ships and a force of 110 sailors and 553 soldiers. On board his ships were also sixteen horses, creatures never before seen by the Aztecs.

Cortés and his men arrived off the coast near present-day Veracruz and went ashore. They were immediately visited by Montezuma's representatives who, believing the Spaniards to be gods, brought gold and other valuable offerings. This convinced Cortés that he had found the opportunity to make his fame and fortune. Intent on conquering these new lands for Spain, Cortés ordered the ships burned. Now there was no choice but to press forward.

The governor of Cuba had not given him the power to conquer Mexico, but Cortés was ambitious. He avoided the governor's limitation by founding the new city of Veracruz on the coast of Mexico, then appointing one of his soldiers to be the governor. This new governor then granted Cortés the power to conquer Mexico in the name of the king of Spain.

When explorer Hernán Cortés (pictured) landed in Mexico in 1519, the Aztecs mistook the Spaniard for the benign god Quetzalcoatl, who, they believed, had returned from his long exile.

THE CONQUEST OF MEXICO

At that time the Aztec realm included five to six million people and dozens of small city-states in addition to the Aztec capital of Tenochtitlán in the Valley of Mexico. Cortés had fewer than a thousand men. How could such a small band of soldiers conquer the mighty Aztec empire?

To begin with, Montezuma believed that the Spaniards were gods whose arrival was predicted by the Aztec religion, a belief that gained further support when the Indians saw the sixteen horses. The Aztecs described the mounted horses as four-legged monsters with human bodies growing from their backs. Furthermore, the bows and arrows, spears, darts, and clubs of the Aztecs were no match for the steel armor, muskets, swords, knives, crossbows, and ten cannons of the Spaniards.

But perhaps the greatest advantage for Cortés and his men was the long-smoldering hatred that the millions of Indians who were brutally controlled by Tenochtitlán felt toward the Aztecs. Cortés also had another stroke of good luck.

The Indians who lived on the Gulf Coast gave Cortés many valuable gifts but none so valuable as a young woman named Marina. She became an advisor and interpreter to Cortés as well as his mistress and mother of his son. She helped him understand where the Aztecs were most vulnerable, and as a reward she lived her later years in great honor and riches in Spain. Today Marina is considered a traitor and the Mexican people refer to her as Malinche. Now when someone acts in a treacherous way, Mexicans say that person is *malinchismo*.

With Marina's help, it was not difficult for Cortés to convince many of the subjugated people of Mexico to join him in fighting their Aztec rulers. Taking full advantage of the situation, he built up an army of thousands of Indians recruited from the many groups who hated the Aztecs.

The Aztec capital was built on a group of islands in a large lake. In his first attack on Tenochtitlán, Cortés and his band simply crossed the broad causeways that led across the lake and into the capital. Taking advantage of Montezuma's trust and hospitality, the Spaniards seized the Aztec king. After a series of battles during which Montezuma was killed by his own people, the tide began to turn against Cortés. Retreating from his fortified position within the city, Cortés and his men fled over the main causeway across the lake. Loaded down with looted treasure, many of the Spaniards were killed by

XOCOATL, THE TREAT OF THE GODS

In 1519, the Aztec ruler Montezuma still believed Cortés was the returning god Quetzalcoatl. Believing this, the trusting Montezuma served a bitter drink to Cortés and his men that was ordinarily reserved for the Aztec nobility. This beverage, served with cinnamon and honey, was made from the pods of the xocoatl plant, which was found only in the New World. Cortés liked the drink, and after he introduced it to the courts of Spain it gradually spread throughout Europe and eventually the world. Meanwhile the pronunciation of the difficult Indian word for the drink's main ingredient became "chocolate."

To this day Mexican hot chocolate is usually made with cinnamon, a combination that goes back to preconquest Indian civilizations. For centuries the Europeans made hot chocolate the same way the Aztecs did, roasting, fermenting, grinding, and brewing the beans from the pods of the xocoatl plant, better known in English as the cacao plant.

Aztecs shooting arrows at them from canoes. The remains of the Spanish force escaped and regrouped in an area where the local people were more friendly.

Cortés immediately began devising a new plan for conquering Tenochtitlán. He knew he could not depend on using the causeways in an invasion, so, even though the Aztec capital was seventy-five hundred feet (2,286 meters) above sea level, Cortés started preparing for a naval battle. He gathered up every bit of metal, rigging, and sailcloth that remained from the eleven ships he had burned at Veracruz, and had his men cut enough lumber for thirteen small ships. Meanwhile reinforcements and more horses arrived from Cuba. Then with the help of eight thousand friendly Indians, he transported all these materials over the mountains and to the edge of the lake that surrounded Tenochtitlán.

By the end of April 1521, Cortés had finished construction of the warships. Many Indian war canoes were added to the fleet. When Cortés looked at his invasion force, he saw thirteen warships with cannon, a fleet of war canoes filled with armed Indians, 928 armored Spanish soldiers (84 horsemen, 650 foot soldiers with swords and shields, and 194 others armed with crossbows and muskets), and thousands of Indian warriors on foot. The time had come to begin the final siege of Tenochtitlán.

Outmaneuvered, their food and drinking water cut off, their ranks reduced by smallpox and other diseases introduced three years earlier by the Spaniards, the Aztecs still

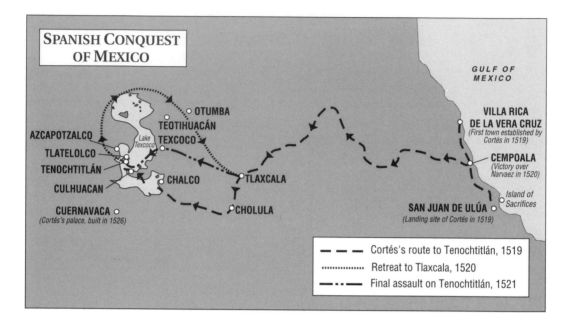

withstood the intense siege for ninety days. Then the Spaniards captured young Cuauhtemoc, the new—and last—Aztec king. That seemed to demoralize the defenders, for soon after Cuauhtemoc's capture, the capital fell. On August 13, 1521, the Spanish conquistadors entered Tenochtitlán.

Over the still-smoldering ruins of the once proud and beautiful Aztec capital, a new city began to rise. Symbolizing the future of Mexico, a Catholic cathedral was built on the stones of the demolished temple of the Aztec's god of war and the sun, Huitzilopochtli. That cathedral is still in use in the heart of modern Mexico City.

EXPANSION OF SPANISH RULE

From the new Spanish capital built on the ruins of Tenochtitlán, Cortés sent expeditions in all directions to conquer other Indian groups, explore the territory, establish gold and silver mines, and continue the search for a sea route to India and Asia.

After conquering the Aztecs, Cortés moved quickly to control the other Indian tribes in southern Mexico. During the course of this campaign of subjugation, the Spaniards burned all the Aztec books and records they could find. This effectively destroyed thousands of years of Indian learning in architecture, mathematics, and astronomy. Then in 1524

Cortés ordered Cuauhtemoc, who was still being held prisoner, to be hung on suspicion of inciting revolt among the Indians. Using such ruthless methods, the Spaniards extended their rule as far south as Guatemala and Honduras by 1525.

The Mayans proved to be excellent guerrilla warriors and gave the Spanish a tough time. The Yucatán peninsula remained a Mayan stronghold for twenty years, and in some parts of the interior the Mayans successfully resisted the Spaniards for another 150 years.

At first the Spaniards routinely enslaved captured Indians. In 1537, however, the Catholic Pope issued a bulletin discouraging slavery. From then on Spain's approach to the Indians changed from conquest to pacification. This policy of pacification formed the basis, at least theoretically, of the New World mission system.

Not all of the Spaniards treated the Indians with cruelty or disdain. Friar Bartolomé de las Casas, who arrived in New Spain (as the Mexican territory was then called) in 1531, dedicated his life to defending the Indians. He also wrote a book describing the atrocities committed by the conquistadors that was read in Europe. Until his death in 1566, Friar Bartolomé used his position as a king-appointed missionary in a mostly futile effort to gain justice and respect for the Indians.

Spanish friar Bartolomé de las Casas denounced the conquistadors' cruel treatment and enslavement of Indians in New Spain.

The first Spaniards to move into the arid and less populated northern reaches of New Spain were Franciscan and Jesuit priests who established a string of mission fortresses. Using religious conversion, or when that failed, military might, the Spanish attempted, with varying degrees of success, to control the nomadic Indians who frequently raided the expeditions sent to search for precious metals.

The Spanish search for New World riches found its greatest success in silver. In 1540 they discovered a huge silver deposit in the present-day state of Zacatecas followed over the next twelve years by major silver finds in Hidalgo, Durango, Guerrero, and Guanajuato. Soon New Spain began minting its own silver coins.

Following Cortés's retirement, New Spain was placed under the control of a viceroy appointed by the king of Spain. Military expeditions from New Spain pressed into Texas and what is now the U.S. state of California in a race for North American territory with other European powers, specifically France, Britain, and Russia. By the end of the sixteenth century, Spain claimed much of what is today Texas, California, Arizona, New Mexico, Nevada, and Colorado for New Spain.

REVOLUTION
AND TROUBLED
INDEPENDENCE

By the end of the sixteenth century, the Spaniards claimed most of what is today Mexico. Governing the new colony, however, was a good deal more difficult than claiming it. New Spain was a very large piece of territory; it was a great distance from Europe; and its huge and often resentful population could rise up in armed rebellion at any time.

In one way Spain's problems were soon simplified. All over the land that would one day be called Mexico, Indians were dying. They had no immunity against diseases introduced by the conquistadors, and they were treated harshly by most of their Spanish masters. Consequently, during the first two centuries of the colonial period (from 1519 when the Spaniards arrived to about 1700) the Indian population fell from about twenty-five million to just one million.

THE ROLE OF THE CATHOLIC CHURCH
DURING THE COLONIAL PERIOD

The Catholic Church moved rapidly during the early years of New Spain to convert the surviving Indians to the European faith. Through the efforts of resourceful and dedicated missionaries, around one hundred thousand churches and convents were constructed during the sixteenth century alone. Built with Indian labor and primitive tools and techniques, thousands of these striking architectural accomplishments remain in use all over Mexico today.

From the earliest days of New Spain, the church and the government worked hand-in-hand. In many places church officials *were* the local government. As a result, the Catholic Church came to dominate the economy of New Spain, until, by the close of the colonial period, it owned more than half

An ornate eighteenth-century Catholic church crowns a hilltop in Taxco, Mexico. During the colonial period, missionaries diligently worked to convert New Spain's Indians to Catholicism.

the land and buildings in Mexico. Since church property was not taxed, this meant half of the country's real wealth was not producing any income for the national treasury.

During the colonial period, from the conquest to 1821, New Spain developed rapidly in several ways. The world supply of silver actually doubled during this time as the result of the rich mines in New Spain. Huge ranches called haciendas became immensely productive. As a result of these two developments, there arose a small but wealthy and influential group of criollos (pure-blooded Spaniards born in the New World, also called creoles).

At that time, all the officials in New Spain were gachupines (pure-blooded Spaniards born in Europe). Since Spanish law forbade criollos from holding government posts, a major conflict between the criollos and the governing gachupines was inevitable. Furthermore, anger and resentment had been building for a long time in the poor classes as the result of the continuing oppression of the Indians and the growing Indian-Spanish mestizo population. A revolution was brewing.

MEXICO'S FIRST REVOLUTION

In 1776, the American Revolution set an example for all European colonies in the Western Hemisphere. The French Revolution, which soon followed, added more fuel to the growing fires of revolution that were sweeping through the criollo population of New Spain. Spain attempted to prevent "dangerous ideas" about independence from spreading to the colony, but angry criollos managed to smuggle in the writings of Rousseau and other French revolutionary thinkers. Dozens of secret groups sprang up where the members discussed the new revolutions. It was in these groups that the criollos formed the first solid resistance to the hated economic policies of the gachupines. In particular they resented being forced to sell the products of the mines and haciendas to Spain while being prohibited from free trade with other countries.

Although millions of mestizos and Indians suffered because of the inequalities of New Spain's extremely class-based society, it was the criollos and a few priests who began the movement for independence from Spain. In 1804 Spain's King Charles III, fearing the church was becoming too powerful, decreed that all church funds be turned over to the king. At that time the church had been serving as a bank to the criollos, so when the gachupines forced the priests of New Spain to call in the loans they had made to the haciendas, great hardships were caused for the criollos. Then in 1808, Napoleon Bonaparte invaded Spain, leaving the gachupines temporarily without support from Spain. The angry priests and the resentful criollos began planning a revolt.

Mexico's struggle for independence from Spain began on September 16, 1810. In the town of Dolores in the province of Guanajuato, a fifty-seven-year-old parish priest named Miguel Hidalgo y Costilla issued an emotional plea known as the *Grito de Dolores* (Cry of Dolores). Hidalgo's *Grito* called for the end of Spanish rule, for equality of the races, and for redistribution of land from the rich to the poor. Mexican Independence Day (September 16) celebrates this event.

HIDALGO AND THE CRIOLLOS JOIN FORCES

Hidalgo, now considered one of the founding fathers of Mexico, was a well-educated, courageous humanitarian. He was sympathetic to the Indians, which was unusual among

Mexican clergymen. Against gachupine law, he began teaching the Indians agricultural methods and pottery making. This irritated the Spanish viceroy to no end, and he planned to punish Hidalgo.

Meanwhile all across New Spain, groups of criollos were plotting to overthrow the gachupines. In Queretaro a group of renegade army officers, led by Ignacio Allende, emerged as the center of the criollo movement. They wanted to avoid a military action and bloodshed by convincing the army to end their allegiance to the gachupines and declare New Spain's independence from Spain. Hidalgo had formed close ties with this group, so when Allende learned that the viceroy intended to arrest the priest, he made sure Hidalgo heard about it.

With trouble brewing, Hidalgo responded with his impassioned *Grito de Dolores*. He quickly organized an army of angry mestizos and Indians, not realizing how the hatred that had been simmering for centuries in these oppressed people would change the character of the revolution.

Led by Hidalgo and Allende, and under a banner depicting the Virgin of Guadalupe, the Indian and mestizo forces headed toward Mexico City to kick out the gachupines. Armed with clubs, slings, axes, knives, machetes, and their hatred of their oppressors, the ragtag revolutionary army descended on Mexico City.

INDEPENDENCE

The revolutionaries attacked with a vengeance, and even the Spanish artillery could not prevent the mass slaughter of gachupines that followed. Hidalgo was shocked by the extent of the violence. He had not foreseen the bloodbath when he made his hasty and emotional decision back in Dolores.

The bloody victory was short lived, however, and the rebellion was crushed by the viceroy in 1811. Hidalgo and Allende were executed by the gachupines thus ending the first of the revolutions and civil wars that were to wrack Mexico for seventy-five years.

Almost immediately one of Hidalgo's associates, another mestizo priest from the southern state of Guerrero named José Maria Morelos, took up Hidalgo's cause. Whereas Hidalgo's campaign had been largely based on hatred of the Spaniards, Father Morelos planned his moves with cold

Father Hidalgo (on horseback) rallies Indians and mestizos to join his 1810 revolution against Spanish rule.

logic. He defined specific goals for the revolution, most important of which were a freely elected government, prohibition of class distinctions and slavery, and a fair taxation system. He formed a militia and succeeded in winning a lot of territory in the south.

In 1813 Morelos convened a congress at Chilpancingo which led, a year later, to a formal declaration of independence for the areas under his military control. Unfortunately for Morelos, just then Napoleon retreated from Spain, which meant that the king could now afford to send more troops to New Spain. After five years of brilliant military actions, Morelos was captured and the reinforced Spaniards crushed this second rebellion. In Mexico City on December 22, 1815, Morelos was shot by a firing squad.

Following Hidalgo's crushing defeat, mestizo priest José Maria Morelos (pictured) led his own revolt, winning much territory in southern New Spain.

Then in 1820, a rebellion in Spain threatened the country's conservative privileged class, including the gachupines in New Spain. For the first time, they began to think of declaring their independence from Spain. Their desire to break with Spain had nothing to do with building a just society for Indians, mestizos, and criollos. Rather, the gachupines were simply trying to preserve their position of wealth and power in the New World.

Meanwhile, despite the execution of their top leaders, bands of guerrillas were keeping the ideals of Hidalgo and Morelos alive, and the scheming gachupines intended to use this to their advantage. Rebellious gachupine leaders appointed Agustín de Iturbide, a first generation criollo sympathetic to their cause, to lead New Spain's loyalist troops. Then Iturbide announced to the Spaniards that remained loyal to the king that he was taking his troops out into the country to wipe out the last guerrillas. His true mission, however, was to make contact with the current guerilla leader, Vincente Guerrero, and make plans for a new independence movement.

In 1821, Guerrero, Iturbide, and the gachupines presented Spain with the *Plan de Iguala* that was designed to avoid a war, and Spain, in its weakened state, agreed to this document. It declared that the Mexican nation would now be independent from Spain, that its religion was Roman Catholic, and that its inhabitants were to be united without distinction between Mexican and European. The part of the *Plan de Iguala* that convinced Spain to sign was the provision for a representative of the Spanish monarchy to head the constitutional government in Mexico City. But by the time the king's representative, Juan O'Donojú, arrived in Mexico, the combined troops of Iturbide and Guerrero controlled most of the country and a new document, the Treaty of Cordoba, eliminated the Spanish. O'Donojú was forced to sign the Treaty of Cordoba on August 24, 1821, thus officially ending New Spain's dependence on Old Spain.

During the eleven years of bloodshed from Hidalgo's call to arms in 1810 to the Treaty of Cordoba in 1821, six hundred thousand Mexicans died in the fighting. Despite this tragic cost, decades of despotic rulers, political unrest, and more wars still lay before the new nation.

Santa Anna and War with the United States

Mexico was now an independent nation, but internal struggles continued between those who wanted Mexico to be a republic and those who wanted it to be ruled by a king. After independence, those who wanted a king succeeded in appointing Iturbide emperor. His reign only lasted two years before he was overthrown by another revolution that established *Los Estados Unidos de Mexico* (the United States of Mexico). A new constitution in 1824 provided for a federal republic with nineteen states, four territories, and a federal district. It also abolished slavery and gave all males, including Indians, the right to vote. In reality, however, restrictive laws made it almost impossible for most of the poor Indians and mestizos to actually vote.

After so many years of fighting, the new country's economy was teetering on bankruptcy. Anti-Spanish feeling had driven out most of the Spaniards and with them the majority of the trained people in the country and their money. This began a half century of a vicious cycle: Whenever there was too little money to pay the military, the officers revolted, captured the government, borrowed money from other countries at high interest rates, used money that could have gone to education and social programs to pay the interest on the high-risk loans, and soon the government was broke again. Then there was another revolution.

Following independence, the people of Mexico badly needed a leader who could bring order and unity to the country, one who could start the Mexican nation on a path of building, class reconciliation, and economic growth. What they got instead was Antonio López de Santa Anna. At the end of his twenty-five years in government, Santa Anna had not achieved a single accomplishment for the welfare of the country. During the same period, Mexico lost over half of its territory to the United States.

Santa Anna, a criollo, was an ambitious army general in charge of enforcing the expulsion of Spanish

Agustín de Iturbide, the gachupine turned-emperor, ruled Mexico for a mere two years before being overthrown by a new revolution.

troops when, in 1833, he seized power and revoked the Constitution of 1824. Between 1833 and 1855, he was in and out of the presidency an astounding eleven times. During his military career and intermittent terms as president, Santa Anna managed to fight on both sides of almost every issue of his day.

In 1821 the northern Mexican province of Texas had been settled by three hundred American families led by Stephen Austin. By 1831, the non-Mexican population outnumbered the native Mexicans and the Texans began to talk of independence. In 1835 the Texans declared their independence from Mexico. Santa Anna responded by leading an army of six thousand soldiers to put down the revolt. He defeated the Texans at the Alamo in San Antonio, but during a later battle at San Jacinto, the Texans beat the Mexicans and took many captives. They thought that Santa Anna had managed to escape until they discovered him among the prisoners masquerading as an enlisted soldier. Santa Anna was forced to grant the Texans independence with the Velasco Agreement in 1836.

Criollo general Antonio López de Santa Anna seized the presidency in 1833. During his turbulent twenty-five years in government, Santa Anna served as president eleven times.

After his loss to the Texans, the Mexican government exiled Santa Anna and refused to recognize the Velasco Agreement. The "independent republic" of Texas, as far as Mexico was concerned, still belonged to Mexico. Nine years later, in defiance of a condition of the Velasco Agreement, the United States admitted Texas to its union. Mexico immediately declared war.

Though not all Americans favored war with their neighbor (for example, Congressman Abraham Lincoln strongly opposed it), most of the country was in love with the idea of manifest destiny. This notion declared that all the land from coast to coast was "manifestly" destined to be a part of the United States. Such expansionist thinking overruled the opponents of the conflict, and the United States went to war with Mexico.

Santa Anna was recalled from exile to recruit and lead an army to fight the United States. His poorly prepared and underfinanced troops went north to protect the border. Led by General Zachary Taylor, U.S. forces invaded northern Mexico. Taylor defeated Santa Anna in the Battle of Buena Vista where both sides suffered tremendous casualties. Next,

U.S. troops lay siege to the coastal city of Veracruz on March 26, 1847. During the Mexican-American War, the United States fought to obtain territories from its southern neighbor, including Texas.

MEXICO'S BOY HEROES

With the Mexican-American War reaching its climax, the most formidable obstacle standing between General Winfield Scott's troops and Mexico City was the fortress on Chapultepec Hill. At that time the Mexican Military Academy was located in the fortress, so when the Americans attacked Chapultepec, many of the defenders were young cadets.

As the American troops stormed the hill, the boys from the military academy fought fiercely to protect their country's capital. As the tide turned in the Americans' favor, the soldiers, men and boys alike, fought to the end. One thirteen-year-old confronted an American bayonet charge and was killed as he reloaded his musket. Another young cadet lowered the Mexican flag to keep it from falling into the hands of the enemy and ran across the roof of the fortress. Struck by a bullet, the youngster plunged off the roof to the rocks below, still clutching the flag.

Mexico honors the young cadets as *Los Niños Heroicos*—the heroic children—with a large monument at the foot of Chapultepec Hill in Mexico City.

Dedicated to Los Niños Heroicos, *this monument pays tribute to the young military cadets who bravely defended Mexico's capital during the Mexican-American War.*

U.S. soldiers under General Winfield Scott invaded Veracruz on Mexico's Gulf Coast. Santa Anna's exhausted troops rushed to defend but were defeated again at the Battle of Cerro Gordo. From there the American forces marched, overcoming fierce resistance, to Mexico City and captured the capital on September 14, 1847. After two years of fighting, all of it on Mexican soil, the Mexican-American War was finally about to end.

THE TREATY OF GUADALUPE HIDALGO

Sporadic fighting continued until the Treaty of Guadalupe Hidalgo officially ended the Mexican-American War on February 2, 1848. Financially depleted and beaten to submission, Mexico was further humiliated by this treaty. It forced Mexico to surrender all the territory north of the Rio Grande (essentially Texas) and to sell to the United States (for a meager $15 million) all the land from the Gila River across the Colorado to the Pacific, including present-day California, Nevada, Utah, Arizona, and parts of Wyoming, Colorado, and New Mexico.

Somehow Mexico had not tired of Santa Anna yet, and in 1853 he elevated himself to the position of dictator. He even issued a decree that he was to be addressed as "His Most Serene Highness." Santa Anna saw that he needed to raise funds (mostly for his army), so in 1854 he sold the United States another large piece of Mexican territory south of the Gila River that added area to the present-day states of Arizona and New Mexico. This $10 million deal came to be known as the Gadsden Purchase and represented the last significant boundary change of the Mexican Republic.

After the Gadsden Purchase, Santa Anna could claim the distinction of having lost for Mexico 51 percent of its national territory.

Most historians now agree that the United States provoked Mexico into the war so the Americans could gain more land in the Southwest. When Abraham Lincoln was elected president of the United States, he referred to the Mexican-American War as "the most unjust war there ever was."

BENITO JUÁREZ AND *LA REFORMA*

Benito Juárez was the first real leader of Mexican liberals. The opposite of Santa Anna in every respect, Juárez was a full-

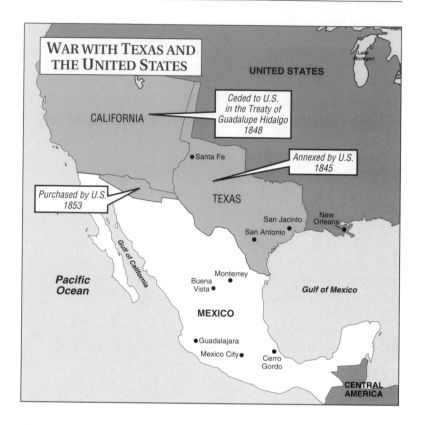

blooded Zapotec Indian, an educated lawyer, and a middle-class liberal. At this point in Mexican history, the term "liberal" was used to mean anticlerical. Although Juárez was certainly a religious man, he was against the political and economic power that the Catholic Church wielded in Mexico.

After serving in several government positions, Juárez had gone into self-imposed exile as a protest to Santa Anna's reign. During that time he lived in New Orleans with a group of other Mexicans who were planning for the country's future once the dictator was gone.

When a liberal rebellion ousted the pompous Santa Anna for the final time in 1854, Juárez returned to Mexico. He was appointed minister of justice in the new government during which time he began the movement known as *La Reforma* (the Reform). The goals of *La Reforma* were to reduce the economic power of the Catholic Church, remove church control of education, marriage, and burials, to force the church to sell all properties not used directly for worship, to foster economic development, and to establish a single standard of justice.

BENITO JUÁREZ AND ABRAHAM LINCOLN

The historian Henry Parkes praised Benito Juárez for displaying a moral quality unequaled in Mexico's history. Known as a stern and unsmiling man, Juárez was deeply religious and dedicated to the cause of justice. He preserved his country during civil war and foreign invasion. His guiding principle in domestic and foreign relations, "Respect for the rights of others means peace," is as valid today as it was in his time.

Born in the southern state of Oaxaca in 1806, Juárez spent his childhood herding sheep. A pure-blood Zapotec Indian, he first studied to be a priest, but later became a lawyer. He served several terms in the state legislature of Oaxaca and then went on to the national congress before being elected governor of Oaxaca. Following Santa Anna's final exit from Mexico, Juárez became minister of justice under the new president Comonfort.

In many ways he has been compared to his contemporary in the United States, Abraham Lincoln. Lincoln was born in 1809 on a poverty-stricken farm in Kentucky. Both men were liberals, and each was to drastically alter the course of his

country. Though they never met in person, they exchanged letters during Lincoln's presidency. When news of Lincoln's assassination reached Juárez, he mourned the loss of a friend and kindred spirit.

The liberal administration of revolutionary statesman Benito Juárez was marked by both reform and rebellion.

The reform movement led to the successful passage of a new constitution, the Constitution of 1857. Advancing the anticlerical ideals of *La Reforma,* this constitution was bitterly opposed by the church and the military, and in 1858 civil war broke out between the conservatives and the liberals. The conservatives captured Mexico City where they set up a new government. Juárez and his liberal supporters had to flee to Veracruz where they set up an alternate government. Fighting continued for three years until the liberals finally succeeded in ousting the conservatives from Mexico City. On New Year's Day in 1861, the liberals made their triumphal return to the capital. Juárez was elected president and immediately reinstalled the Constitution of 1857.

The conservatives, however, did not give up. England, Spain, and France were angry about Juárez's temporary refusal to repay Mexico's foreign debt while the country tried to recover from its bankrupt condition. The conservatives saw this as an opportunity to enlist the help of Europe in regaining control of Mexico. After secret negotiations, the conservatives succeeded in getting England, Spain, and France to send warships to Mexico as a show of force to get Mexico to pay its debts, and pave the way for the conservatives to return to power.

FRANCE INVADES MEXICO

Though England and Spain only wanted Mexico to resume payments on their loans, the emperor of France had other ideas. Napoleon III, the nephew of Napoleon Bonaparte, knew that the United States would oppose a European presence in the New World, but at this point the Americans were occupied with their own civil war. So Napoleon III declared that he would create a "Latin League" to stop the advance of American "manifest destiny." When Spain and England recognized that Napoleon III had more in mind than collecting a debt, they withdrew.

Napoleon III sent a huge army under General Elie-Frederic Forey to Mexico. The French soldiers landed at Veracruz and immediately headed for the capital. Though the Mexicans fought bravely and defeated the first wave of the French invaders on May 5, 1862, near the town of Puebla, ultimately they could not withstand the assault of the French forces. On June 10, 1863, Forey and the French army captured Mexico City, less than sixteen years after the United States had captured it. Soon much of central Mexico was under French control and Juárez was forced to stay on the run in northern Mexico.

When Napoleon III felt that his troops had the country sufficiently under control, in 1864 he persuaded the young and idealistic Maximilian, archduke of Austria, to serve as emperor of Mexico. To the frustration of the conservatives who thought Maximilian would support their agenda, the new emperor began installing liberal reforms. Maximilian was an honorable man, but Napoleon III had left him in the dark about the true state of affairs in Mexico. During the three years of his rule, the young emperor seems to have honestly believed that the people wanted him, but to the Mexicans he was an alien intruder.

When the American Civil War ended, the United States began pressuring Napoleon III to pull his troops out of Mexico. Furthermore, France was being threatened by Prussia and Napoleon III needed his troops at home. The French began withdrawing from Mexico, and soon Juárez and his recruits

CINCO DE MAYO

When the disciplined and well-financed troops of Emperor Napoleon III invaded Mexico in 1862, the country was broke and disheartened from a three-year civil war. Furthermore the country was still deeply divided along the class lines that had caused the civil war.

On May 5, 1862, an outnumbered and outgunned army of mestizos and Zapotec Indians under General Ignacio Zaragoza defeated the French invaders in a brutal day-long battle at the town of Puebla. Though the French came back a year later and took over Mexico, the Battle of Puebla gave the Mexican people the courage to fight back against foreign domination, and eventually they did succeed in driving the French from the country.

The holiday that now commemorates the May 5, 1862, Battle of Puebla is simply called Cinco de Mayo—the Fifth of May. Cinco de Mayo celebrates the resolve of Mexicans to be forever free, to determine their own destiny, and never again to fall to a foreign power. In that spirit Cinco de Mayo is very much like the Fourth of July in the United States.

Because of this similarity in spirit to the American Independence Day, many people in the United States wrongly equate Cinco de Mayo with Mexican Independence which was on September 16, 1810, nearly a fifty-year difference. Interestingly, Cinco de Mayo is celebrated on a much larger scale in the United States than it is in Mexico.

During French rule of Mexico, Maximilian, archduke of Austria, briefly served as emperor. After the Mexicans revolted against the French, Maximilian was captured and executed.

were able to defeat the remaining French forces. Maximilian could not be persuaded to leave. He was captured by the Mexicans and shot.

The French invasion had accomplished what nothing else had been able to bring about: It fused the people of Mexico into a nation.

From Juárez to the Next Dictator

In 1867, Juárez was once again elected president of the nation. He attempted to reduce the national debt by encouraging the growth of industry and commerce. Under his leadership the national railway from Veracruz to Mexico City was completed, and he ordered thousands of schools to be built. Juárez also realized that the miliary was both the country's greatest expense and the greatest threat to a democratic government, so he dismissed forty thousand officers and soldiers, which did little to endear him to the army.

In 1871 Juárez ran for a fourth term. He was opposed by Sebastian Lerdo and an army general named Porfirio Díaz. No one of the three received a majority of the votes so the election went to the congress to decide. Congress named Juárez president again, and Lerdo was named to head the supreme court. A part of the army followed Díaz in an attempted coup, but they were quickly defeated.

The following year Juárez died of a heart attack, and congress selected Lerdo to succeed him. When, in 1876, Lerdo announced he would run for a second term, Díaz ran against him and was elected. Díaz became president of Mexico on November 21, 1876, a post he was to hold, except for one four-year term, until May 24, 1911.

4

DICTATORSHIP, REVOLUTION, AND ONE-PARTY RULE

Mexico's first great leader, Benito Juárez, was as interested in bringing a free democratic government to Mexico as he was in improving the prosperity of everyone in the country. Soon after his death, however, Porfirio Díaz took over Mexico, and for the next three decades he systematically sacrificed democracy and freedom in favor of economic gains for a minority of the country's citizens.

THE PORFIRIO DÍAZ DICTATORSHIP (1876–1911)

Porfirio Díaz, a mestizo from the Mixtec area of the southern state of Oaxaca, was an uneducated man who nevertheless became a clever and ruthless ruler of Mexico. When he first came to power he was a liberal, meaning he was an opponent of the church's excessive power and a supporter of the economic policies introduced by Juárez. That is where the similarities between the two men ended.

Díaz wanted to improve the prosperity of Mexico's upper class, even if this meant everyone else became poorer. Díaz would abide no interference in his plans, so he immediately took steps to suppress troublesome citizens. To Díaz, maintaining public order meant increasingly harsh treatment of anyone who spoke out against his policies. His most visible critics were the protesting Indians and striking mestizos of Mexico's rural areas, all of whom he characterized as bandits.

To put down the various troublemakers, Díaz created a private police force known as the Rurales. The Rurales, recruited from thugs and real bandits, amounted to a private army. They were paid well, provided with handsome uniforms, and authorized to shoot on sight. For the duration of his rule, Díaz used the dreaded Rurales to ruthlessly control Mexico's rural areas.

Some groups resisted the dictator's policies with more determination than others. The fiercely proud Yaqui Indians from the northwestern state of Sonora were a prime example. In response to their defiance, Díaz ordered all able-bodied Yaqui men to be inducted into a special part of the army. This was merely an excuse to force them into slavelike labor. A large number of Yaquis were moved from their homeland in Sonora to sisal plantations in Yucatán or tobacco plantations in Oaxaca where they were used as cheap labor for the wealthy landowners. Those Yaquis who refused were hunted down and shot as "traitors" by the Rurales.

As his regime became more and more oppressive, Díaz moved from his liberal (anti-church) position to a conservative (pro-church) position. He began allowing the church, which had been reduced in power by the Reform Laws installed by Juárez, to function as it had in the past, including owning land beyond the basic needs of the church, influencing local politics, and loaning money.

The government's harsh suppression of opponents made the country appear peaceful to outside observers, despite the resentments simmering beneath the surface. With Mexico at peace for the first time in many years, at least on the surface, the government could successfully attract foreign investment for economic development.

Until Díaz brought in a financial genius named José Ivés Limantour to head the country's treasury for the last sixteen years of his dictatorship, Mexico's national treasury had remained empty and the country's foreign debt had continued to grow. These conditions were discouraging foreign companies from investing in Mexico. Limantour gathered around him a group of brilliant young lawyers, economists, and intellectuals who became known as *los científicos* (the scientists). Limantour and his *científicos* were responsible for the improvements in Mexico's economy under Díaz. Foreign companies were brought in to work the long-neglected mines, to exploit the rich oil deposits, refine sugar, and build factories. As a result the fledgling

Ruthless dictator Porfirio Díaz ignored the needs of the poor during his quest for economic development.

railway system begun under Juárez grew until it covered the country. Foreign trade increased to ten times what it was when Díaz came to power. At last Mexico was able to pay its national debt.

In the eyes of the world, and perhaps a quarter of the Mexicans, Díaz had brought political and economic stability to Mexico. The dictator was praised at home and abroad as an enlightened ruler, the savior of Mexico.

But apart from the industries established and controlled almost entirely by foreigners, Mexico had gone backwards. Most people at that time still lived outside the cities, and rural Mexico had become, once again, a feudal agricultural society.

RIPE FOR REVOLUTION

Between 1883 and 1894, Díaz sold 134.5 million acres (54.5 million hectares) of public land to wealthy speculators and personal friends for only nine cents an acre. He also ordered the lands that had been worked for centuries by Indian communities (called *ejidos*) to be distributed to wealthy landowners. Most of the private lands in Mexico at that time were owned by fewer than one thousand rich families, the owners of the largest haciendas.

By the end of the Díaz regime, the hacienda system dominated the rural areas of the country. While a relatively few wealthy families owned 90 percent of the land in Mexico, 85 percent of the rural population was landless. There were 8,245 haciendas, many of them enormous. Each hacienda was a kingdom unto itself, and they were primitive kingdoms. Since the farming methods employed by the haciendas were based on cheap human labor, there was no incentive to make farms more modern and efficient.

Most of the people in rural areas had no choice but to work and live on these haciendas where they were treated like agricultural slaves. These peasants toiled long hours and were forced to obtain the necessities for their wretched lives at the hacienda store on credit. The workers were always in debt to the haciendas, and their debts were passed on to their children when they died. Landless, yet chained to the land by debt and ignorance, millions of Mexicans were ripe for revolt.

Unrest was building in the cities too. Secret radical and liberal political groups began to emerge, and eventually they formed the heart of a movement known as the *Regeneracion* (Regeneration). Protests and labor strikes led by the *Regeneracion* were put down by Díaz in bloody fashion. This created another focal point of growing resistance to the dictator.

An opening in Díaz's wall of repression and control was needed if a revolution was to even get started, and the eighty-year-old dictator inadvertently created that opening himself. One day, in a mellow mood, he told an American journalist that he was ready to retire and would do so in 1910, the next election year. This statement was intended only to give the impression to readers in the United States that Mexico was, after all, a genuine democracy. But no sooner had the article appeared in print than it was translated into Spanish and circulated widely in Mexico. Mexicans cheered the news.

Francisco Madero, a mild-mannered liberal from one of the largest landowning families in the state of Coahuila, accepted Díaz's statement as truth and announced that he would be a candidate for the presidency in 1910.

As expected, Díaz went back on his statement to the American press and declared that he would be running for an eighth term after all. Madero did not back down and started his campaign as the first legitimate opponent to Díaz in decades. Madero was no fiery revolutionary: He was soft-spoken and small of stature (only five feet, two inches, or 159 centimeters, tall). As a result, the dictator Díaz did not take this challenger seriously. Everywhere Madero campaigned, however, enthusiastic crowds showed up to support him. Díaz got nervous and had Madero arrested on false charges until the campaign was over. No one was surprised when the election was proclaimed in the dictator's favor.

TIERRA Y LIBERTAD: THE MEXICAN REVOLUTION OF 1910

Madero was released from jail after the election. He immediately fled to Texas where he began organizing the overthrow of the Díaz regime. On November 20, 1910, in San Antonio, Texas, Madero declared the presidential election null and void and called for a general insurrection. That date is now observed as the Day of the Mexican Revolution.

Pro-Madero demonstrations sprang up in various parts of the country, but they were quickly crushed by Díaz. At first it seemed that Madero's call to arms was not going to produce much of a response. Then Madero and his supporters heard

Despite his victory over unpopular Porfirio Díaz, liberal Francisco Madero (pictured) was unable to quell unrest among guerrilla rebels and was murdered shortly after assuming the presidency.

about an uprising in the state of Chihuahua that had successfully challenged federal troops. This revolt had been led by a storekeeper named Pascual Orozco and a colorful bandit-turned-revolutionary named Doroteo Arango, better known as Pancho Villa. Madero joined Orozco and Villa, using money from his family's fortune to supply the rebels with arms. The Revolution of 1910 was on.

While Villa and Orozco pressed the revolution in the north, trouble was also brewing for Díaz in the southern state of Morelos. There, a dedicated agrarian leader named Emiliano Zapata had built up an army of Indian and mestizo farmers to resist the local landowners who had repeatedly seized *ejido* lands to increase the size of their haciendas. When Zapata heard Madero's call to rise against Díaz, it was an easy decision to join the revolution. In March 1911, Zapata's tiny force took the city of Cuatla and blockaded the road to the capital.

With rebellion breaking out all over Mexico, Díaz resigned and, in May of 1911, the old dictator slipped quietly away to live his final days in luxury in Paris. Madero was elected president the following October. The revolution seemed to have come to a quick conclusion, but in fact the struggle had just begun.

Zapata asked Madero to return seized lands to the *ejidos*, but Madero refused and insisted that Zapata and his guerrillas disarm. Zapata responded by preparing the Plan of Ayala declaring Madero incapable of fulfilling the goals of the revolution. This plan also demanded the return of stolen land to the *ejidos*, a goal represented by Zapata's famous revolutionary cry "*Tierra y Libertad*" (Land and Freedom).

A VIOLENT POWER STRUGGLE

Zapata, Villa, and other rebels began their own war against Madero. In 1913, after Mexico City had been shelled for ten days, causing heavy civilian casualties, General Victoriano Huerta, one of Madero's own men, betrayed him and arrested Madero and his vice president, José María Peño Suárez. Soon after their arrest, Madero and Suárez were murdered, shot while supposedly attempting to escape, and Huerta assumed the presidency. Madero's overthrow and assassination took place with the knowledge and very likely the assistance of the United States ambassador to Mexico, Henry Lanc Wilson, in direct defiance of President William Taft's instructions to him to stay out of Mexico's domestic politics.

Following the deaths of Madero and Suárez, Zapata once again visited Mexico City. When Huerta also showed no interest in supporting the Plan of Ayala, Zapata went back to Morelos and resumed his revolutionary attacks against the federal government and the haciendas, pushing north toward the capital.

Meanwhile in the north of Mexico, Villa resumed his attacks on the haciendas. At the same time a farmer named Alvaro Obregón put together a force composed mostly of fierce Yaqui Indians to attack government troops in Sonora. Venustiano Carranza, the conservative governor of Coahuila, joined Obregón and Villa as they began a push south toward Mexico City.

Huerta was doomed, not only by the revolutionary forces closing in on him, but also by the election of Woodrow Wilson as president of the United States. As soon as he was elected, Wilson recalled Henry Lane Wilson (no relation), the scheming ambassador to Mexico who had given so much help to the dictators in defiance of the U.S. government's orders.

President Wilson also opened the U.S. border to shipments of arms and ammunition for Villa and Obregón (weapons

WOMEN IN THE MEXICAN REVOLUTION

All Mexicans were touched by the violence of the revolution, but women were particularly affected. Many lost their husbands, sons, fathers, homes, and livelihoods.

But the women of Mexico were not content to simply be victims of the war. It is unlikely that the women of any epic struggle in any age have played a more heroic role. Some women joined the revolutionary forces. Some served as spies or arms smugglers. Others became *soldaderas.* On foot or in freight cars, they accompanied their men from battle to battle, foraging for food, preparing meals, nursing the wounded, bolstering morale, and, in some cases, dying like the soldiers they were.

Rifle-bearing women revolutionaries pose for a photograph during the Mexican Revolution.

bought with cattle Villa stole from the haciendas). Then, as a show of support for the anti-Huerta forces, the United States landed troops at Veracruz and occupied the city.

Obregón's forces reached Mexico City before Villa and his men. Huerta hastily fled the country. Villa was enraged at losing the race to Obregón, especially since Obregón had decided to support Carranza's group. Villa declared Mexico City to be his enemy and refused to meet Obregón or Carranza there.

Since Obregón was not eager to support the Plan of Ayala either, Zapata formed a short-lived union with Villa. Together they stormed the capital and forced Obregón to withdraw. Obregón soon struck back and drove the rebel forces from the capital. He then decided to chase down and destroy his former ally, Villa. Villa and his men loaded the remains of their army onto northbound freight cars and tore up the tracks behind them as they fled to Sonora. Obregón's pursuit was relentless, but slow, as he repaired the train tracks as he went. In the north, Villa's men were slaughtered in a battle

Rebel general Emiliano Zapata (seated, center) and his staff. In an effort to oust Alvaro Obregón from the capital, Zapata joined forces with the infamous Pancho Villa.

"FROM THE HALLS OF MONTEZUMA . . ." — INVADING A NEIGHBOR

The United States has twice invaded Mexico. Both times American forces landed at Veracruz on the Gulf of Mexico. The first time, during the Mexican-American War, U.S. forces pushed all the way to the country's capital, Mexico City, and occupied it. The route taken by the marines and army to Mexico City was the same route Cortés had taken to Tenochtitlán to overthrow Montezuma.

Cortés ultimately conquered most of the land that is present-day Mexico. During the Mexican-American War, the Americans succeeded in grabbing a little over half of the country. To this day Mexicans harbor resentment over this tremendous loss of territory to their neighbors to the north.

with a force led by a grim-faced mestizo named Plutarco Elías Calles from the state of Sonora, a man who would later become president of Mexico.

After Villa lost most of his men fighting Calles, the United States recognized Carranza as the president of Mexico and cut off Villa's supply of arms and ammunition. He was down, but not out. Villa gathered a small band of men and began raiding American property across the border. In 1916 Villa and his men stopped a train in New Mexico and murdered sixteen Americans in an attempt to force a local shopkeeper to deliver weapons for which he had already been paid. In retaliation, President Wilson sent troops under General John J. Pershing across the border in pursuit of Villa. Pershing and his five thousand cavalrymen chased the bandit for almost a year, but Villa repeatedly eluded the Americans. In the process Villa became a larger-than-life folk hero.

Carranza, meanwhile, was struggling to organize a workable government. The Constitutional Convention he convened in Querétaro in December of 1916 was dominated by Obregón. Zapata and Villa were not invited. On February 5, 1917, the new constitution was adopted, and it is the constitution that governs Mexico today.

The Constitution of 1917 was, by-and-large, a confirmation of the Constitution of 1857, but with certain important changes. Article 27 of the new constitution struck at the heart of the hacienda system by incorporating Zapata's ideals for land reform and a return to the *ejido* system. The limitations on the power of the church that began with the 1857 constitution were also included in the new constitution. Influenced by fresh ideas from recent European social legislation, the new constitution called for the government to take a larger role in the social, economic, and cultural welfare of the people. And, very important, the new constitution reasserted the Mexican national ownership of subsoil resources, including oil.

As expected, Carranza was the first president to be elected under the new constitution. When Carranza refused to honor some of his campaign promises, Zapata vowed to oppose him. Carranza's soldiers set up an ambush, and they shot and killed Zapata in 1919.

Villa met his end in 1923 when he, too, was ambushed and killed while running more raids into the United States.

When Carranza continued to refuse to enact social reforms, allies of Obregón forced the president to flee. He was assassinated in 1920 in Veracruz as he attempted to flee with five million pesos in gold.

With Carranza gone, Obregón became president. In 1921, which is now considered the year when modern Mexico began, Obregón began the long process of restoring peace to the country that had been torn apart by revolution for almost

Pancho Villa (fourth from right) and his men display their stockpiles of arms and ammunition. Villa and his band started raiding cities north of the border after the U.S. government shifted its support from Villa to President Carranza.

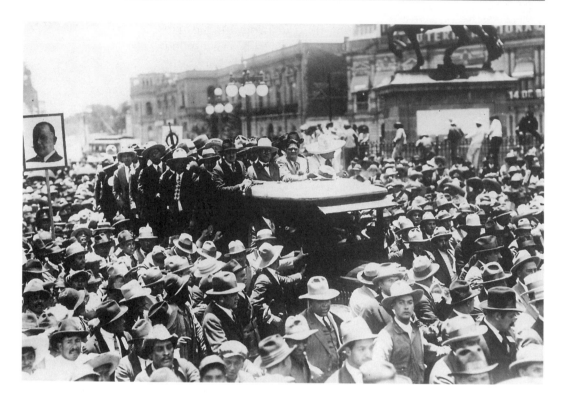

Supporters crowd the streets of Mexico City to witness General Obregón's triumphant entrance to the capital. Obregón became president in 1921.

a decade. He immediately began acting on the provisions of the Constitution of 1917, especially the land reforms. He put in place the machinery to return communal land holdings to the villages (*ejidos*). Educational and cultural reforms were also resumed.

The long struggle of the Mexican Revolution was finally over. It had helped to define the modern Mexican nation and give Mexicans a sense of identity and purpose, but at a tremendous cost. Millions of Mexican citizens had died in the fighting. Tens of thousands had fled the violence and settled in Texas or California. The economy was in a shambles, and in every city and town there were countless homeless and starving people.

POST-REVOLUTIONARY MEXICO

Rebuilding Mexico after the revolution took nearly twenty years. Obregón managed to hold on to the presidency for four years. He was followed in 1924 by Calles, who had been Obregón's ally in the battles with Villa in Sonora. Calles continued the same programs based on the Constitution of

1917, including an acceleration of the *ejido* program. He also began pressuring foreign petroleum companies who owned the country's oil reserves (as the result of deals they had made with Díaz) to accept leases instead of outright ownership. The oil companies resisted with what most Mexicans considered an arrogant disdain for their justified and patient demands, and the foreign companies continued to control Mexican oil.

During Calles's term, he enforced the new constitution's anticlerical measures that Obregón had ignored. This caused the church to retaliate by suspending all religious ceremonies, but what led to violence was the declaration by the archbishop of Mexico that Catholics could not accept the constitution. A church-supported rebellion known as the *Cristeros* exploded in western and central Mexico where

ZAPATA SPEAKS

Mexico's great revolutionary leader Emiliano Zapata could attack with words or guns. Here, in a letter to the new president who had turned his back, in Zapata's view, on the revolution, words were the weapon of choice. The letter is excerpted from *The Course of Mexican History* by Meyer and Sherman.

As the citizen I am, as a man with a right to think and speak aloud, a peasant fully aware of the needs of the humble people, as a revolutionary and a leader of great numbers . . . I address myself to you, Citizen Carranza. . . . From the time your mind first generated the idea of revolution . . . you conceived the idea of naming yourself chief . . . you turned the struggle to your own advantage and that of your friends who helped you rise and then share the booty—riches, honors, businesses, banquets, sumptuous feasts. . . .

It never occurred to you that the Revolution was fought for the benefit of the great masses, for the legions of the oppressed whom you motivated . . . a magnificent pretext . . . for you to oppress and deceive. . . .

In the agrarian matter you have given or rented our haciendas to your favorites . . . and mocked the people in their hopes.

hundreds of innocent people died. Mediation by the U.S. ambassador to Mexico, Dwight Morrow, helped to end this violent chapter in the church-state controversy.

Calles ruled with an iron hand, and, as he became more and more dictatorial, he changed the constitution to allow a president to be reelected (as long as the terms were not consecutive). He also increased the presidential term from four to six years. By making these changes, Calles's intention was to pave the way for Obregón's reelection in 1928.

Obregón was indeed reelected in 1928, but he was assassinated by a religious fanatic. That same year the reelection of presidents was banned and the presidential term was set at six years, a policy that continues to this day in Mexico.

Since he could not be reelected, Calles formed the *Partido de Nacional Revolucionario* (PNR, National Revolutionary Party) to appoint short-term presidents to fill out Obregón's term, presidents who were sympathetic to the values of the PNR. When the next elections came around in 1934, the party offered as their candidate the revolutionary general, Lázaro Cárdenas. Since there was no organized opposition to the PNR, Cárdenas was elected president.

Cárdenas, a mestizo with Tarascan Indian heritage, began to strengthen the labor union movement in defiance of

Plutarco Elias Calles became president of Mexico in 1924. Calles's strict dictatorship upheld the Constitution of 1917, but it also expanded the presidential term and enabled presidents to be reelected, although not consecutively.

Calles and other powerful figures in the National Revolutionary Party. When Calles objected, Cárdenas forced him into exile.

CÁRDENAS AND THE RISE OF MEXICAN NATIONALISM

Cárdenas proceeded to reorganize the PNR into a structure where the candidates for every important political position in the country were selected by the party and then offered for "election" without any significant opposition. With power thus assured, Cárdenas continued to push forward with the goals of the Constitution of 1917, particularly by seizing land from wealthy owners and redistributing it to *ejidos*.

Lázaro Cárdenas proved to be a strong president. Through his leadership, Mexico eventually gained its economic independence.

The PNR organization has continued to the present day, although after World War II the name was changed to the *Partido Revolucionario Institucional* (PRI, the Institutional Revolutionary Party).

Meanwhile, the foreign companies that owned Mexico's oil industry, mostly British companies, had still not taken the hints to trade their ownership for leases. On March 18, 1938, Cárdenas took over the petroleum industry and set up a government-owned company, Petróleos Mexicanos (Pemex), to run it. Britain immediately broke off diplomatic relations with Mexico. For a moment it seemed that Britain and the United States (American oil companies also lost property in the seizure) might go to war with Mexico. Then United States president Franklin D. Roosevelt urged Mexico to make prompt and fair payment for the properties they had seized, and if Mexico agreed to do so, he would not attempt to enforce the claims of the oil companies.

With Mexican nationalism at an all-time high, the country set about raising the money to pay the oil companies for their losses in Mexico. No contribution was too small, no sacrifice too great. Women donated their jewels, schoolchildren their lunch money. Eventually the oil companies agreed to accept $113.5 million in compensation, and even though it took until 1962 to pay off this debt, Mexico owned its oil again. Mexicans now celebrate March 18 as the anniversary of the country's economic independence.

MEXICO DURING WORLD WAR II

During World War II, Mexico helped the United States in its war effort by supplying materials and labor. The scarcity of imported goods in Mexico also forced the country to increase domestic production. In addition, Mexican troops fighting in the Pacific for the Allies needed materials, both imported and domestic. All these war-related factors fostered increased trade between the United States and Mexico, and brought the two countries closer together.

During this period, the Mexican economy grew and the country took advantage of its increasing prosperity to build new universities and technological training and research centers.

MEXICO AFTER WORLD WAR II

Since the Cárdenas period, Mexican history has been one of small and subtle shifts as leaders have sought to "institutionalize" the revolution. In practice what this has meant is that for sixty-eight years the Institutional Revolutionary Party (PRI) won every national election. This domination by the PRI had several beneficial results for the country. Presidential successions were as peaceful as they were predictable. In 1953 the PRI backed an initiative to give women the right to vote (the first election in which they voted was in 1958), and in 1970 the voting age was lowered to eighteen. Steady growth in foreign trade and industrialization helped to create a sizeable middle class, and Mexico became a major oil and gas producer. But life under the PRI was not always pleasant.

In 1968, thousands of students took to the streets of Mexico City to demand the liberalization of the political system. Their protests reached a peak in October on the eve of the Mexico City Olympic Games, the first time the Olympics were ever held in a Spanish-speaking country. With the entire world watching, President Gustavo Díaz Ordaz responded to the students' demands for a freer system with gunfire. At the Plaza of Three Cultures in Mexico City, federal troops fired on a huge demonstration. Hundreds of young people were killed in a massacre that lasted four hours. The government claimed that snipers fired first and the military was only responding to protect the people, but ABC and NBC news videotapes showed the troops opening fire in response to nothing worse than hurled rocks and curses. This tragedy produced open and widespread criticism of the PRI's brutal and authoritarian rule for the first time in the party's history.

Mexico's economic growth in the 1970s was financed with international loans totaling almost $80 billion. Government planners calculated easy repayment of these loans with the income from huge oil reserves discovered in 1976 in the southern states of Chiapas and Tabasco. What they had not planned on was the excess in world oil production of the early 1980s and the sharp fall in oil prices. Mexico found itself unable to pay even the interest on its loans and a severe financial crisis engulfed the country in the 1980s. Unemployment and inflation combined with a sharp drop in foreign investment caused terrible suffering for all but the very rich. Furthermore, the problems with the economy put more cracks in the previously impenetrable wall of the PRI's power.

In September 1985, an earthquake devastated Mexico City, killing an estimated seven thousand people and destroying hundreds of buildings. The government's slow and

NAZIS IN MEXICO

The *Unión Nacional Sinarquista,* from the Spanish *sin,* without, and *anarquia,* anarchy, was a Mexican political party founded in 1937 by Hellmuth Schleiter, a German professor of languages teaching in Guanajuato state. Unknown to most Mexicans, Schleiter was a Nazi and a German intelligence agent. At that time the power in Mexico was based on the anti-church revolution, so the *Sinarquismo,* as the party was called, in an effort to undermine the government, called for an increase in the power of the Roman Catholic Church. This Nazi-backed organization opposed communism, liberalism, and the United States while supporting the European fascist movements led by Hitler, Mussolini, and Franco.

In 1941, at its peak, the *Sinarquismo* claimed one million members. As the Mexican economy improved, the attraction of the movement faded and its numbers declined. After the war a new political party, the *Partido de Acción Nacional* (PAN), recruited agrarian reformers from the declining *Sinarquismo.* Today PAN does not represent any Nazi beliefs, and in fact it is a pro-business party. In the 1990s, PAN would present the first real threat to the power of the PRI.

Students march through the streets of Mexico City on August 13, 1968, demonstrating against the current political system and calling for reforms.

inadequate response to this disaster brought strong criticism for President Miguel de la Madrid. That, and an alleged national election fraud in 1988, raised to new levels the criticism aimed at the PRI and the antidemocratic, increasingly conservative, one-party system it represented. The dominant position of the PRI was beginning to crumble.

Then in the 1988 presidential elections, Cuauhtémoc Cárdenas, the son of former president Lázaro Cárdenas (the man

who nationalized Mexico's oil industry) left the PRI to run as
the candidate of an independent group of leftist organiza-
tions. When it became clear that the PRI candidate was falling
behind Cárdenas in the early returns, the PRI-controlled
computerized vote-counting system allegedly broke down.
The next day the PRI candidate, an ambitious Harvard-
educated economist named Carlos Salinas, was declared the
winner. The truth about the vote count will probably never
be known because the ballots were incinerated by Salinas's
government in 1992.

Most Mexicans were convinced that the 1988 election had
been stolen from Cárdenas by the PRI. Immediately following the election, tensions were extremely high everywhere in
the country. At that point, as historian Enrique Krauze wrote,

*Supporters of Cuauhtémoc
Cárdenas rally in Mexico
City on November 11, 1988,
to protest the upcoming
inauguration of president-
elect Carlos Salinas.*

"An order from [Cárdenas] would have sent Mexico up in flames." Instead, Cárdenas took the nonviolent path and sought justice in the courts.

After losing in the courts (lack of evidence), in 1989 Cárdenas formed the *Partido de la Revolucion Democratica* (PRD, the Democratic Revolutionary Party) which united renegade PRI members and other opponents of the dominant power. Cárdenas then spent the following years crisscrossing Mexico and focusing his energy on the nation's impoverished majority.

After taking office in 1994, President Ernesto Zedillo reformed the election process despite the wishes of PRI hardliners.

Carlos Salinas appeared to be working hard to get the country's economic chaos under control, and at first it looked like he was succeeding. He was a popular and charismatic leader and the people tended to believe it when he said Mexico was finally going to join the modern nations of the world. Beneath the surface, however, the improvements were only skin deep, and when Salinas left office in 1994, the truth came out.

As Salinas left office, the PRI's economic policies of the previous six years caused a huge peso devaluation. Overnight Mexicans found themselves earning about half of what they had been making even as prices shot sky-high. The ensuing financial collapse plunged Mexico into the worst depression it had known since the 1930s. More than two million jobs were lost, food prices and interest rates soared, and thousands of small businesses closed.

Furthermore, the *ejido* system, the cornerstone of the Mexican Revolution, had been crippled by Salinas, making the plight of the country's poor farmers even worse. In the final analysis, only the rich had prospered under Salinas, and as he left office Mexico was, once again, virtually bankrupt.

The PRI Loses Ground

In 1994, despite the widespread belief that the elections were rigged, the PRI managed again to get their candidate, Ernesto Zedillo, elected. But the ruling party was reeling. Subsequent investigations revealed that Salinas and his family had amassed a huge fortune during his administration even as the country's economy was falling apart. Disgraced, Salinas went into exile while his brother was jailed for "illegal self-enrichment," a brother-in-law was imprisoned, and another brother-in-law was shot to death. Furthermore, the top general appointed by Salinas to fight Mexico's growing drug trade, Jesus Guitierrez Rebollo, was found to be working for the drug bosses.

Inheriting this mess, Zedillo chose to ignore the PRI's "dinosaurs" (a name used by reform-minded Mexicans of all political persuasions to indicate the PRI hard-liners who want to continue the old corrupt ways of maintaining power). To his credit, Zedillo installed strict new safeguards for the election process in an effort to restore public confidence.

While the electoral process changed for the better under Zedillo, the PRI apparently did not. In the 1997 elections for various mayors and governors, the PRI harassed political commentators, blocked international funding from human rights groups attempting to monitor the elections, and openly purchased votes in rural areas. What is worse, between 1989 and 1997, more than 470 members of the PRD were killed, and reporters investigating PRI corruption continue to be kidnapped and beaten, and sometimes killed. Most of these crimes remain unsolved.

The widespread anger at Salinas and the PRI gave new life to Cárdenas, the PRD, and other political parties. In 1997, the first elections held after Zedillo's electoral reforms were in place showed just how far the PRI had slipped. Cárdenas ran for mayor of Mexico City (the second most powerful position in the country with twenty-three million people and all of the important ministries and institutions based there) and was elected by a landslide. What is more, the voters elected five non-PRI state governors and stripped the PRI of its congressional majority for the first time in its sixty-eight-year history. With pride and hope, Mexicans embraced what was being called the first true Mexican multiparty democracy.

THE LAND OF THREE CULTURES—THE PEOPLE AND INSTITUTIONS OF MEXICO

Because of the three distinct influences that shape almost every aspect of Mexican life, Mexico has been called the land of three cultures: the Indian culture derived from the Aztecs and other indigenous peoples of Mexico; the old world European culture and religion, especially that of Spain, which arrived with the conquistadors in the sixteenth century; and the modern culture shaped by technological and industrial influences from the world at large, twentieth-century changes within Mexico's society and government, and the relentless pressure of a growing population.

Mexicans are fully aware of the contributions of these three cultures. Not far from Mexico City's main plaza (the *Zócalo*) may be found another square known as *La Plaza de las Tres Culturas* (the Plaza of the Three Cultures). The buildings in and around this plaza symbolize Mexico's three major cultural influences. In the middle of the plaza, representing the Indian influence, are the ruins of an Aztec temple. Nearby, a church built in 1609 by the Spaniards symbolizes the culture of the Spanish conquistadors who destroyed the Aztec civilization. Surrounding the plaza, tall steel and glass buildings emphasize the changes brought by modern culture.

To this day, Indian, Spanish, and modern all exert strong influences that continue to shape Mexico's society, government, architecture, art, and literature. The result is a complex and proud heritage that affects all Mexicans.

The ancient ruins, elaborate cathedral, and contemporary buildings of La Plaza de las Tres Culturas *symbolize Mexico's three main cultural influences: the Aztecs, the Spanish conquistadors, and modern Mexican society.*

AN ETHNICALLY MIXED PEOPLE

Mexico's varied races and ethnic groups are so mixed that the government does not even attempt to keep detailed ethnic statistics. Moreover, recognizing separate racial groupings in Mexico would counter the government's policy of discouraging a caste system.

Castes, social categories that place one racial group above another, are considered a major obstacle to creating a fair and just society. Mexico, however, has had a very class-conscious society since the Spanish conquered the Indians.

In colonial Mexico the most privileged class consisted of the gachupines (Spaniards born in Spain) followed by the criollos (pure-blooded Spaniards born in Mexico), the mestizos (mixed Indian and Spanish blood), and finally the indios (pure Indians). Often the Spanish ruling class simply lumped the indios and the mestizos together as indígenas and treated them all poorly. In modern Mexico pure-blooded Indians still feel the sting of an entrenched, centuries-old system of oppression that treats them as social inferiors. The resulting social injustices and economic inequalities that trap many of Mexico's Indians in poverty have fueled a series of peasant revolutions. In 1994 the latest armed Indian-led revolution began in the poverty-stricken state of Chiapas in southern Mexico.

INDIANS

Though Indians were the country's original inhabitants, today Mexico's pure-blooded Indians are a minority. Consisting of over fifty different groups or tribes, Indians now account for between 10 and 25 percent of Mexico's population depending on how they are counted (the lower figure includes only those who still speak an Indian language, the higher figure includes those with predominantly Indian cultural and physical features). Some of these groups, especially the Nahua, Maya, Zapoteca, Mixtec, Otomi, and Tzeltal, are numerous and comprise the majority of the inhabitants in several areas of Mexico. Other Indian groups have dwindled to a few dozen families and may disappear entirely in the future. While many of Mexico's Indians have gradually absorbed features of the surrounding mestizo culture, some groups, especially in remote mountainous areas, live much as they did when the Spaniards arrived. In some cases they do not even speak Spanish.

Today most Mexicans, regardless of their ethnic background, express pride in their Indian heritage. Every city displays monuments to ancient Indian heroes like Cuauhtémoc (the last Aztec ruler, hung by Cortés) and modern Indian

DIA DE LA RAZA

In the United States, October 12 is known as Columbus Day, but in Mexico it is called *Dia de la Raza*, which translates to "Day of the Race." *Dia de la Raza* celebrates the mixture of cultures and races—the many Indian groups, the Europeans, and the small numbers of Africans and Chinese—that produced the people of modern Mexico.

Mexicans are aware that the Americas were first discovered by their Indian ancestors, so the arrival of the Europeans (represented by Columbus's voyages) has little importance in Mexico except to mark the beginning of the second of the country's "three cultures."

leaders and heroes like the former president of Mexico, Benito Juárez, a pure-blooded Zapotec Indian. And yet Mexico's respect for its Indian heritage does not prevent widespread discrimination against Indians. Despite government programs to improve life among Indian groups, many of Mexico's Indians live impoverished lives with inadequate drinking water, schools, hospitals, and clinics.

THE SPANISH AND THE MESTIZOS

Most of the early colonists from England, Holland, and France who settled in more northern parts of North America arrived in the New World with their families. The Spanish

Today, pure-blooded Indians are a minority group in Mexico and most live in poverty as a result of centuries of oppression.

conquistadors, on the other hand, came to the New World as members of a military operation and they did not bring their families. As a result, intermarriage between Spanish men and Indian women was common in early Mexico. The children born to these Spanish-Indian couples were the first mestizos.

Of all the ethnic groups in modern Mexico, the mestizos are the most numerous. While only 15 percent of modern Mexico's population is of pure-blooded European ancestry, more than 60 percent of the population is mestizo. The mestizos are more than simply a numerical majority. Mexico's mestizos encompass a more complete religious, political, and racial blending than the mixed European-Indian cultures found today in any other former European colony in Latin America.

Despite this blending of cultural and racial elements, Mexico's people are still sharply divided by other differences.

Economic and Social Divisions in Mexico's Population

Mexico's society is sharply divided by income and educational level. Although a significant middle class is rapidly growing in the cities, a huge division remains between the wealthy, well-educated elite and the urban and rural poor.

Nearly 70 percent of the over ninety million Mexicans live in urban areas, specifically Mexico City, Guadalajara, Monterrey, Puebla, Leon, Tijuana, Ciudad Juárez, and in seventy other cities with populations over one hundred thousand. While most of the rural population consists of poor Indians and mestizos, in the cities there exists a class structure based almost exclusively on economic level with little regard to ethnic background.

Members of the upper class, about 2 percent of the population, are characterized by a high level of education, expensive housing, ownership of multiple vehicles and luxury consumer goods, and frequent international travel. Citizens of the upper middle class, about 20 percent of the population, often have a university education and hold professional or managerial positions in the workforce. The lower middle class, about 49 percent of the population, live in average homes and spend a greater portion of their incomes on the basic necessities. The remainder of the population includes the rural, the underemployed, and the unemployed poor.

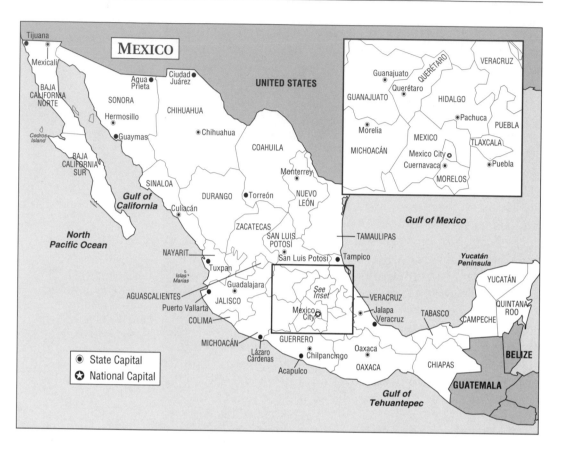

EDUCATION, HEALTH CARE, AND WELFARE

In Mexico education is free for children between the ages of six and sixteen. There is a national goal to provide everyone with a minimum of nine years of schooling, but in rural areas this is seldom achieved. Attendance is mandatory, though school authorities lack the manpower to enforce this rule. Each day about 15 percent of all school-age children do not attend school.

Although the average Mexican attends school for only five years, according to government statistics the nation's literacy rate has risen to about 85 percent in 1996, up from 70 percent in 1970.

Most schools in Mexico are run by the government, but there are also many church-run schools, especially at the secondary level. The government also runs schools especially for Indians where Indian teachers conduct classes in both Spanish and native Indian languages.

Primary (elementary) education lasts six years. Primary schoolchildren begin classes at 8:00 A.M. and finish at 1:00 P.M. It is common for older primary schoolchildren in urban areas to work at jobs in the afternoon after school.

Secondary education consists of a basic three-year curriculum followed by another three years for those students intending to go to a university. In many areas secondary schools offer students a choice of two attendance times, morning (7:30 A.M. to 1:30 P.M.) or afternoon (2:30 P.M. to 8:30 P.M.).

In general the best schools in the country are located in the larger cities. There are about fifty universities in the country and ten of these are in Mexico City. The country also has several hundred professional, vocational, military, and technical colleges. Though less than 10 percent of Mexicans receive advanced education, most Mexicans consider a college degree to be a passport to economic and social success.

The main obstacle to the government's efforts to bring education to all Mexican citizens has been the astounding growth in the country's population. Since the 1940s Mexico's population has grown 50 percent faster than the world average (roughly three times faster than the United States). In

Schoolchildren in Guanajuato, Mexico, wear matching uniforms. School attendance is mandatory for children between the ages of six and sixteen.

Between classes, students visit with friends on the campus of the University of Iberioamericana in Mexico City. The nation's capital is home to ten different universities.

1996 the population was about four times what it was in 1940, and more than half of Mexico's people are under the age of twenty. With such accelerated growth, the government has found it impossible to keep up with education and other basic services to the people.

Education for all is not the only hope thwarted by the rapidly increasing size of the Mexican population. Health care and help for the poor and unemployed has not kept up with the growing population. Government-subsidized health care and social assistance have greatly reduced the previously high death rate in Mexico, but the health of the majority of the country's population, the poor people, is still far below minimum international standards. Malnutrition and the associated health problems of rickets, vitamin deficiency, and anemia are very common among the poor of Mexico.

The government plans to eventually have medical and hospital care available to all citizens. Rural clinics attended by at least a nurse exist throughout most of the country, but it is often a day's journey for Indians in remote areas to reach the nearest clinic.

Mexico presently has no unemployment benefits and only a tiny welfare program. Estimates indicate that as many as 60 percent of all Mexicans are unemployed or underemployed. To survive, a person who does not have a job must rely on the help of family members, or in some cases, the Catholic Church.

RELIGION

Mexico's constitution guarantees separation of church and state so there is no official religion, but Roman Catholicism is practiced by about 90 percent of the population.

Before the Spanish conquest, the Indians of Mexico worshiped gods whom they believed would provide rain and good harvests. Over a period of thousands of years they built great temples and pyramids to honor their gods who could be generous or cruel.

YOUNG PEOPLE IN MODERN URBAN MEXICO

Many young people living in Mexican cities today have more in common with their age group in American cities than they do with rural Mexican youth. A major difference between the youth of the two countries is that city kids in Mexico are generally far more aware of political issues than American kids. In fact the big changes in Mexican politics are largely driven by the eighteen-to-thirty-year-old voters who totally distrust the PRI.

Most city kids in Mexico finish high school and many go on to higher education. They scoop up American products like Gap jeans and McDonald's burgers. They listen to rock, rap, and reggae. They watch popular American movies.

Mexican city kids are more liberated than any generation before them. They leave home and get their own apartments before marriage, something unheard of just a generation ago. And they aren't afraid to leave their home towns for jobs in distant cities. Breaking out of traditional cultural patterns is not without its problems, however.

AIDS is the third leading killer of Mexicans under age thirty-five. Now the country's young are demanding a more honest and open discussion of topics like sexuality in the traditionally prim media. Demands by young Mexicans for more realistic and relevant media have led to a rebirth of Mexican television, radio, film, and journalism.

Despite their increased awareness and better opportunities for education, Mexico's young city dwellers are facing an unemployment rate that is twice as high as that of older people. Furthermore, 40 percent of people under thirty live in poverty, a situation that has never before existed in Mexico. Youthful poverty and unemployment are the main reasons for the increasing numbers of young Mexicans crossing the border to look for work in the United States.

Today, young people from Mexico's cities comprise the most liberated group in the nation's history.

With the Spanish conquistadors came missionaries to convert the Indians to Roman Catholicism. Considering that the Indians were practicing a complex group of religions that were thousands of years old, these tough and determined missionaries were surprisingly successful. The Indian belief in many gods played right into the Catholic tradition of many saints. Furthermore, the missionaries were clever enough to build their churches on or near Indian temples and allow their converts to keep some of their earlier beliefs. As a result, many of Mexico's Indians still practice their preconquest religious beliefs even though they have been converted to Catholicism, and they frequently mix the two in their ceremonies. More often, however, the Indians believed that their gods had also been defeated by the Spaniards and accepted the god of the conquerors.

Catholicism is firmly established in Mexico, but the country's constitution contains several anticlerical provisions intended to limit the church's former political and economic power. No doubt the framers of Mexico's constitution were thinking of the church's long history of exploiting and oppressing Indians, and how, during the Mexican Revolution,

Catholic missionaries erected churches throughout Mexico during the colonial era. Although Catholicism remains the primary religion in Mexico, the church no longer wields political or economic power.

some church officials in Mexico had sided with Spain. Still, the overwhelming Catholicism of the voters makes modern political leaders reluctant to enforce these constitutional laws.

Though the Catholic Church is no longer a strong political or economic force in Mexico, religious beliefs are still a very important part of Mexican life. Today most of Mexico's practicing Catholics, even in the upper and middle classes, practice a form of folk-Catholicism that incorporates elements of ancient Indian religions and local legends.

In urban areas of Mexico, church attendance by Catholics has dropped in recent years. The numbers of Mexican Protestants, Jews, Mormons, and Mennonites, however, are growing. Only 3 percent of Mexicans describe themselves as nonreligious.

LANGUAGES

Mexico is the largest Spanish-speaking country in the world. Spanish is the official language and is spoken by 95 percent of the population.

Similar to the way that the English spoken in the United States is different from the English spoken in England, Mexican Spanish is different from that spoken in Spain. The type of Spanish spoken in Mexico is often called "Latin-American Spanish" to distinguish it from the Castillian Spanish of Spain. Furthermore, Mexican Spanish has many differences from other Latin American versions of Spanish. Most notable are the great number of words that come from Indian languages. During the twentieth century many English words have also crept into the average Mexican's vocabulary.

In addition to Spanish, about fifty different Indian languages with almost a hundred dialects are spoken in Mexico. The most common Indian language is Nahuatl, essentially the same language spoken by the Aztecs. It is estimated that almost 10 percent of Mexico's Indians do not speak Spanish.

SPORTS

Mexicans love sports, and without a doubt the country's most popular sport is soccer. Many Mexican baseball players have gone on to play in the American major leagues, and baseball has become almost as popular as soccer. Mexicans also love to participate in or watch the national style of rodeo called *charriadas*.

Mexican Olympic teams have won medals in many fields, and the country's tennis players routinely rank high in world standings. And, with so much coastline, it should not have come as a surprise when a Mexican boat and crew won the first round-the-world sailboat race. Mexican boxers have competed well internationally, too. Mexico also has produced several world champions of jai alai, an indoor game similar to handball that has been called the fastest ball game in the world.

BOOKS, MOVIES, AND FOLK ART

A long line of Mexican poets, dramatists, novelists, and political writers have enriched the literature of Spanish-speaking people and the world at large. While a number of Mexican writers have received acclaim in the twentieth century, the country's literary heritage goes back to at least the seventeenth century. One of the most famous early Mexican writers was a Catholic nun named Sor Juana Inés de la Cruz (1651–1695). Her poetry is considered to be among the finest ever written in the Spanish language.

Mexico's modern writers have found considerable acceptance and success outside of Mexico as well as in their native land. These include Octavio Paz, Samuel Ramos, Carlos Fuentes, Mariano Azuela, Juan Rulfo, Laura Esquivel, and Agustin Yáñez. In 1990, Paz became the first native-born Mexican to receive the Nobel Prize for literature (awarded for his overall contributions to literature through essays, drama, and above all, poetry). His most famous work is a book-length series of linked essays, *The Labyrinth of Solitude: Life and Thought in Mexico,* which examines the character of the Mexican people while seeking to link the Mexican experience with all humanity. Fuentes, the author of *The Old Gringo* (which was made into a movie in the United States) and many other acclaimed books, often speaks to audiences outside Mexico about his country's history and current cultural changes.

The subject of Mexican literature often includes discussions of the great "mestizo dilemma"—the national sense of being caught between the worlds of the Indian and the European. This experience of duality appears in another recent trend in Mexican literature known as magic realism, in which the real-life details of a peasant existence are combined with

Mexican Catholicism and the Virgin of Guadalupe

Mexican Catholicism is as different from European Catholicism as Mexican Spanish is different from the language spoken in Spain. A number of important aspects of the Catholicism practiced in Mexico are found only there, and these variations are often closely linked to preconquest Indian religious beliefs.

Perhaps the most famous variation, found all over Mexico, is the cult of the Virgin of Guadalupe. In 1531 a dark-skinned Virgin Mary appeared three times to an Indian peasant named Juan Diego at a place near Mexico City that had once been a sacred Aztec temple dedicated to the goddess Tonatzin. The Virgin commanded Diego to collect roses and present them to the local Catholic bishop with a request to build a church in her honor. Diego collected the roses and wrapped them in a blanket. When he unfolded his rose-filled package, he and the bishop saw an image of the Virgin imprinted on the cloth. This was declared a miracle, and a shrine was built in the Virgin's honor.

The Virgin of Guadalupe is considered to be the patron saint of all Mexicans, and the official feast day of Guadalupe, December 12, is a major holiday throughout the country. On that day millions of Mexicans make a pilgrimage to the Basilica of the Virgin outside Mexico City to thank her for answering their prayers. Many crawl up the hill to the shrine on their hands and knees. After the Vatican in Rome, the Basilica of the Virgin is the most visited religious site in the Catholic world.

One indication of how important the Virgin of Guadalupe is to the Mexican psyche took place in 1976. That year the Basilica of the Virgin was rebuilt with government financing—this despite the official separation of church and state.

Faithful visitors flock to a shrine honoring the Virgin of Guadalupe, Mexico's patron saint.

longings for escape that turn into dream-like happenings. One of the most popular examples of magic realism is found in Esquivel's *Like Water for Chocolate,* which was made into a Mexican film that was popular both in the United States and Mexico.

Mexico has a large movie industry. Mexican films and movie stars are popular throughout Latin America, and they also play to sizeable audiences in Spanish-speaking areas of the United States.

Mexico's oldest art form is folk art, which is still produced in many parts of Mexico. Mexico's artisans, many of them Indians who practice traditional crafts utilizing ancient design themes, create an enormous variety of folk art. This work takes many forms, including handwoven textiles and clothing, ceramics, glass work, jewelry, leather work, basketry, hats, wood carvings, religious paintings, ironwork, and furniture.

With roots traceable to the country's folk art tradition, Mexico is home to one of the most admired and imitated art forms in the Americas: large, colorful, socially significant murals. Inspired by the country's patriotic, revolutionary spirit, great Mexican artists create their grand works of art on the walls of public buildings throughout the country. The most well known of the muralists are José Orozco, Diego Rivera, and David Siqueiros. With paint, and sometimes mosaic, the murals illustrate and interpret social, historical, and political events in heroic style.

OCTAVIO PAZ ON THE HUMAN CONDITION

Author Octavio Paz is widely known for his insights into the Mexican outlook on life, but, as this passage, excerpted from his book *The Labyrinth of Solitude,* shows, he was also interested in what it meant to be a human being living in any culture.

Solitude—the feeling and the knowledge that one is alone, alienated from the world and oneself—is not an exclusively Mexican characteristic. All men, at some moment in their lives, feel themselves to be alone. And they are. To live is to be separated from what we were in order to approach what we are going to be in the mysterious future. Solitude is the profoundest fact of the human condition.

Renowned for her paintings as well as her stormy love life, artist Frida Kahlo remains a controversial figure in Mexico.

In addition to the muralists, there are a great many fine Mexican painters. One of the more unusual is Frida Kahlo who is as well known for her paintings as for her tempestuous marriage to muralist Diego Rivera and her affair with the Russian social theorist Leon Trotsky. Rufino Tamayo, a Zapotec Indian, was a painter who rejected art as a means of social protest, unlike the politically loaded murals of Rivera and Siqueiros. Inspired by the European Impressionists and Cubists, his work was especially well received in France.

MUSIC

While Mexico's writers and muralists are respected and often loved by the middle and upper classes, Mexico's musicians

HIRING A MARIACHI BAND AT GARIBALDI SQUARE

Almost every city in Mexico has a place where mariachi bands gather and play to each other while they wait for someone to come along and hire them for a wedding, fiesta, or serenade. In Mexico City, the best place to hire mariachis is at Garibaldi Square.

A mariachi group can have anywhere from three to a dozen or more musicians. The members of each band wear matching costumes of fitted pants and jackets decorated with silver ornaments, frilly shirts, boots, sombreros, and sometimes colorful ponchos. Dozens of mariachi bands congregated all in one place, all their handsome outfits sparkling as they play their best songs, create a festive scene in the square.

Mariachis play mostly romantic, sentimental songs. Usually two or more of the musicians sing in harmony while the violins, horns, and guitars accompany them. This is the music played at most Mexican parties, weddings, and public fiestas. It is also a Mexican tradition for a man to hire mariachis to serenade his lover, or for a husband to serenade his wife. In Mexico, the most popular serenading time is between 2 and 4 A.M.!

Members of a mariachi band strum guitars while serenading at a Mexican party.

are loved by virtually everyone in the country. When most outsiders think of Mexican music, they think of the music of the mariachis with their horns, violins, and guitars. Mariachi music originated in the nineteenth century during the French occupation of Mexico. The French desired small bands to play festive music at weddings, and the mariachi group was born. In fact, the word "mariachi" actually comes from the French word for marriage. Originating in the city of Guadalajara in the state of Jalisco, mariachi music is now popular all over the country.

By far the most frequently heard music in Mexico these days is what is collectively known as *norteña,* so named because it originated in northern Mexico. *Norteña* music is a mixture of Latinized polkas and waltzes (brought to Mexico by immigrants from east Europe and Germany), *rancheras* (with roots in Mexican cowboy life), and *corridos* (Mexican ballads).

Mexicans also enjoy a wide range of music beyond mariachi and *norteña.* Traditional Indian and folk music is still played and enjoyed, especially in rural areas. Symphonies and discos both can be found in cities, and the radio and *MTV Internacional* play American-style rock, *technobanda,* salsa, Latino reggae, and Spanish rap.

Looking at the literature, art, and music of modern Mexico, it is tempting to change the "Land of Three Cultures" to the "Land of Many Cultures."

6

MEXICO TODAY

Modern Mexico was born in the blood and fire of the revolution of 1910, a revolution that many people feel continues today. Mexicans face immense challenges, including one of the fastest growing populations in the world, a government riddled with corruption, an explosive influx of drugs not all of which are bound for the United States, and a simmering revolution in the south. To handle these challenges, Mexico has abundant resources and a deep reserve of strength and perseverance in its greatest asset, its people.

MEXICO CITY, THE HEART OF MEXICO
Located in the center of the country, Mexico City (called simply "Mexico" by the country's citizens) vies with Tokyo for the dubious honor of being the world's largest urban center. Originally, this immense metropolis fit within the borders of the country's federal capital (the *Distrito Federal,* similar to Washington, D.C., in the United States), but Mexico City outgrew Mexico, D.F., many years ago. Today, with a population in excess of 24 million (and growing at a rate of two thousand people per day), Mexico City's borders are no longer clearly defined. With the city and its suburbs stretching out in all directions, greater Mexico City now occupies at least nine hundred square miles (2,331 square kilometers) of land in the Valley of Mexico.

All of the achievements of modern Mexico as well as all of the country's overwhelming problems can be seen in the crowded streets of this bustling city. The country's economic heart is here: more than half of its industry, the national stock market (the *Bolsa*), and the headquarters of almost all of the country's banks and big businesses. The national government is located here. The largest and oldest university in the country and the lion's share of technical and vocational schools are here. About twenty daily newspapers are published here and the majority of Mexico's television studios are here.

Despite being Mexico's governmental, economic, and cultural center, Mexico City is one of the most troubled cities in the world. It has grown so large in such a short time that efforts to supply basic needs like plumbing, electricity, and housing have not been able to keep up with the population increase. Air pollution from vehicles and factories has become so bad that chemicals in the air are killing vegetation and ruining old buildings. The surrounding mountains trap this pollution to form some of the worst smog in the world, and the air in the capital is almost unbreathable during many parts of the year.

And yet, October can bring sparkling clear days to this seven-thousand-foot-high (2,134 meters) supercity. Then the *chilengos,* as residents of Mexico City are called, can see the nearby volcanoes against the brilliant blue skies, the same view that the Aztecs of Tenochtitlán had when Cortés arrived. The clear air of October might be seen as a symbol of the events that have recently brought the winds of change to Mexico City. And change in Mexico City means change in the entire country.

A Time of Change

Mexico is struggling under a heavy burden of problems caused by two major factors: an exploding population and a government that has a long history of neglecting the majority

A thick layer of smog enshrouds the skyline of Mexico City. The ever-increasing population in the capital, coupled with the increase in automobiles and factories, has led to dangerously high levels of air pollution.

of the country's citizens while using corruption to enrich those in power. These two fundamental problems have caused or amplified a host of other national problems, including recurring economic crises, unsolved assassinations, free-wheeling drug cartels, soaring crime rates, corrupt politicians and police, and revolution in rural areas. All these problems have their roots in Mexico City.

About 65 percent of Mexico's 95 million people are under age thirty. During the 1997 elections, a third of the registered voters were ages eighteen to twenty-nine. Almost 80 percent of these young people voted against the candidates of the PRI, the only party their parents had ever known. The PRI, infamous for election cheating and frightening opponents, suffered the biggest losses in its long history. Two relatively new parties, the National Action Party (PAN) and the Party of the Democratic Revolution (PRD) pushed the PRI from dominance in Mexico's house of representatives. In the most significant election, the PRD candidate, Cuauhtémoc Cárdenas, was elected mayor of Mexico City (his official title is governor of Mexico, D.F.).

Cuauhtémoc Cárdenas waves to supporters during a campaign rally in Mexico City. Cárdenas was elected mayor of the capital in 1997.

When he became mayor of Mexico City in December of 1997, Cárdenas was faced with as big a set of problems as any mayor of any city in the world has ever had to face, including horrible air pollution, widespread police corruption, extensive housing shortages, rampant crime, and a colossal waste-disposal predicament. By being more successful at managing the chaos of Mexico City than his PRI predecessors were, he will be in an excellent position to be elected president of the country in the year 2000.

THE *EJIDO* SYSTEM TODAY

To understand what is happening in Mexico today, it is necessary to understand the current state of the *ejido* system, the economic effects of the maquiladoras, the North American Free Trade Agreement (NAFTA), and the roots of the Indian rebellion centered in the states of Chiapas and Guerrero.

The *ejido* system has been a cornerstone of every Mexican revolution and continues to form a unique part of the Mexican economy. Mexicans view the *ejidos* as the cultural and economic soul of rural Mexico, the only system that recognizes the worth of the Indians and mestizos who actually work the soil.

This communal farming system—where the people who work the land share its ownership—dates back to the preconquest civilizations. An *ejido* is more than just cultivated fields; it includes school properties, water and forest resources, buildings and facilities, and anything else essential to the collective efforts of its members.

The *ejido* system was protected by the Constitution of 1917, but legislation passed during the Salinas regime severely weakened the program. Even before that, despite the apparent fairness of the *ejido* concept, there were already signs that the *ejido* may not be the answer for modern Mexico.

Soon after the Mexican Revolution of 1910 it began to become clear that the mere possession of a few acres of land by the communal farmers of an *ejido* did not provide a magic solution to the problems of the rural population. Land was part of that solution only when it could be made to produce. Without seeds or modern tools like tractors, and without the money with which to buy them, the average peasant (sometimes called a *campesino* in Mexico) was unprepared to make the land produce.

In the middle of the twentieth century, the government established agricultural banks to furnish the *ejidos* with seed and equipment, and to act as agents for selling the harvested crops. A new emphasis was placed on teaching small farmers better agricultural techniques, diversification, the use of fertilizers, and prevention of soil erosion.

Even with agricultural banks and better farming methods, however, many believe the *ejido* system is destined to ultimately fail. The primary reason given is the limited amount of farmland available. Under even the best conditions, only about a fifth of Mexico's land is potentially suitable for agriculture. With the population continuing to grow, soon there will not be enough land for the growing *ejidos*.

During Salinas's rule, the PRI dismantled the part of the constitution (Article 27) that provided for redistributing land to the *ejidos*. This left a great part of Mexico's most fertile lands, especially in the southern parts of the country, occupied by large cattle ranches and sugar, coffee, and cotton plantations. The mostly Indian farmers in places like Chiapas and Guerrero were forced to farm the thin rocky soils found on the steep slopes of the highlands. These small plots of land were insufficient to support the Indian population, and the poorest of them migrated toward the last frontier in the south, the Lacandon jungle. There the colonists cleared tracts of rain forest land which exposed red clay soils that lose their fertility within one to three crop cycles. Such land soon becomes useless to the farmers and their *ejidos*, and so they clear more rain forest.

As a result of the increasing population, the end to land redistribution, and the economic woes wracking the entire country, the *ejido* system is rapidly disappearing in Mexico. Many of the peasant farmers, unable to feed themselves from their inadequate *ejidos*, migrate to the cities in search of work. All too often their search is without success.

MAQUILADORAS

To provide work for the country's growing numbers of unemployed, the government of Mexico established the maquiladora program in 1965. This plan allows foreign-owned companies to build manufacturing facilities (usually near the U.S.-Mexico border), train Mexican workers, import parts and raw materials, and export the products without being taxed. This program was intended to benefit both the Mexicans (by providing employment and job training) and the companies (who benefited from cheaper labor than in their homelands). American and Japanese companies were especially enthusiastic about the maquiladora system. By 1998, over thirty-five hundred maquilas (factories) employed a total of almost nine hundred thousand Mexicans, and generated around 40 percent of Mexico's US$96 billion in annual exports.

The maquiladora program was eliminated by the North American Free Trade Agreement (NAFTA) of 1994. NAFTA required the special maquiladora tax breaks and tariff exemptions be eliminated at the end of the year 2000. Even without these special privileges, the factories that previously operated under the maquiladora provisions were not expected to close, but the long-term effects of ending the maquiladora program are not yet known.

NORTH AMERICAN FREE TRADE AGREEMENT

The North American Free Trade Agreement (or *Tratado de Libre Comercio*—TLC in Spanish) went into effect in Canada, Mexico, and the United States in 1994. For Mexico, NAFTA recognized the already existing economic reality of the increasing commercial integration that Mexico and the United

States had gradually developed over the preceding 150 years as a result of sharing such a long border. In 1993, for example, fully 80 percent of all U.S. exports went to Mexico, and 71 percent of all U.S. imports came from Mexico.

Supporters of NAFTA say it will stimulate the economies of all three countries by lifting trade barriers and taking full advantage of the production strengths of each nation. Opponents in Canada and the United States, however, feared that many jobs would be lost to Mexico. In a famous statement, former U.S. presidential candidate Ross Perot warned that there would be a "giant sucking sound" as jobs fled the United States to low-wage Mexico. It did not happen; on the contrary freer trade between Mexico and the United States under NAFTA has created many more jobs than it cost according to a 1997 report from the U.S. Labor Department. Furthermore, in the first three years of NAFTA, Mexico-U.S. trade increased by 65 percent despite the devastating 1995 financial crisis in Mexico.

Another side of NAFTA is that it helped create the largest, most independent-minded youth wave Mexico has seen since the 1920s. NAFTA freed up more than just commerce. It increased the flow of ideas across the U.S.-Mexico border and gave young Mexicans access to different standards by which to measure their country. The "NAFTA generation" is already having a major impact on Mexico's politics, culture, and economics. And while this economic "revolution" is taking place in Mexico's cities and industrial centers, the old style of Mexican revolution has reappeared in the south.

NEW VIOLENCE: REBELLION IN CHIAPAS

We have nothing to lose, absolutely nothing, no decent roof over our heads, no land, no work, poor health, no food, no education, no right to freely and democratically choose our leaders, no independence from foreign interests, and no justice for ourselves or our children. But we say enough is enough! We are the descendants of those who truly built this great nation, we are the millions of dispossessed, and we call upon all of our brethren to join our crusade, the only option to avoid dying of starvation!

With those words from the Zapatista National Liberation Army (more commonly know by its Spanish initials, EZLN),

Mexico's latest violent revolution began. On New Year's Eve, 1993, armed EZLN guerrillas simultaneously seized control of six towns in the highlands of Chiapas in the south of Mexico. The guerrillas were almost entirely teenagers and young adults from the region's impoverished Indian populations. Though most of the original EZLN members came from ethnic Mayan groups, their rebellion was not purely an ethnic one.

From the start of the rebellion, EZLN leaders made it clear that they were fighting to improve the lives of all of Mexico's poor people, no matter what their ethnic background. Nevertheless, no area in all of Mexico is poorer than Chiapas. A majority of the Indians there live in dirt-floor houses made of wood slats and mud. According to the Mexican National Institute of Statistics, Geography and Information, 1.25 million Chiapas residents, almost half of all the households, do not have running water (compared to a national figure of 20 percent without running water). In Chiapas more than 30 percent of the state's 3.2 million inhabitants are illiterate compared to 13 percent nationally. Although Chiapas produces 55 percent of Mexico's hydroelectric power, 34 percent of its homes (760,000 people) do not have electricity (nationally 12 percent do not have electricity). And of a total population of 3.8 million in Chiapas, 2.5 million earn less than the equivalent of US$4 a day.

In addition to their extreme poverty, the Indians of Chiapas have long been subject to fierce racism and discrimination on the part of the dominant mestizo society, and this has led to the south of Mexico being largely ignored by Mexico City. Even local officials in Chiapas are PRI loyalists who generally ignore the Indians' claims for land and justice. "The origins of the armed movement in Chiapas are in actions that were stimulated by the government which has for decades ignored the Indians," wrote columnist Miguel Angel Granados Chapa in Mexico City's *Reforma* newspaper.

After generations of discrimination and poverty, few people were surprised that Chiapas and the surrounding areas of Oaxaca and

A Zapatista National Liberation Army guerrilla holds an assault rifle while sitting at his post in the jungle of Chiapas, an area where poverty is extreme among the indigenous population.

Guerrero were the birthplace of a new Mexican revolution. Though the poverty is most extreme in the south, such conditions are familiar all over Mexico. Thus in the years following the initial armed uprising in Chiapas, a new slogan spread throughout the country: "Chiapas is Mexico."

But not everyone believes the PRI government was the bad guy in Chiapas. Federico Estevez, an aide to Zedillo early in his administration, told the *New York Times* in 1997 that

---

 ## FROM THE CHIAPAS FRONT

Mexico's revolutionary tradition continues today. On New Year's Day, 1994, a new rebellion made its violent beginning in the southern state of Chiapas. This eyewitness report by Peter Rosset illuminates some of the reasons behind this revolution.

Michael and I were at home [in Chiapas where they were teaching how to improve agricultural methods] on the first day of 1994 when they say all this began. . . . In the plaza bright, young Indian men, women, and even children, wearing clean and freshly pressed polyester khaki uniforms, sported one-shot rifles, bayonets, home-made grenades, machetes, axes, and AK-47s. We talked with the masked leaders. The message was not new, not a surprise to anyone living here: we want land so we can grow food, access to health care, free schools, a decent wage, an end to racism. Our lives are not worth living if things do not change. . . . The state of Chiapas is a world divided by racism and by rich and poor. A majority of the Mayan Indians here live in wood slat and mud houses with dirt floors. Eight to ten people sleep together in one room on three or four beds. Most have access only to dirty water from a nearby stream for cooking, cleaning, and drinking. . . . On the fifth day of the war we listened to the bombs drop all afternoon while we tended to the seedlings, tucking them into the soil, and gently watering them. All the while the army was at work with their bombs, destroying homes, killing civilians, and forcing others to flee from their communities. How strange to be caring for such fragile little plants while the army was busy destroying human beings. How difficult to understand why a government finds it more convenient to repress and destroy rather than to nurture and educate its people.

the trouble in the south of Mexico was much like the struggle for civil rights in the south of the United States in the early and mid-1960s. He pointed out that even though two of the U.S. presidents at the time, Kennedy and Johnson, were Democrats, as were the governors and most of the local officials in the south, people did not accuse the Democratic Party of wrongdoing each time a civil rights worker was murdered. Andrew Reding, director of the North American Project of the World Policy Institute, responded to this comparison by reminding Estevez that the American presidents sent troops to the south to enforce desegregation laws and protect civil rights workers while Mexican president Zedillo sent troops to protect the PRI governors and to arrest EZLN leaders as common criminals.

Reding has also pointed out that PRI-backed paramilitary groups have been responsible for more than fifteen hundred murders in Chiapas (including the December 1997 slaughter of forty-five unarmed men, women, and children in the Indian village of Acteal while state police stood by) since Zedillo broke the truce with the EZLN. In retaliation, EZLN and other revolutionary groups have ambushed and killed unarmed PRI supporters as well as army and military personnel.

To reduce tensions and moderate inequalities, from 1994 to 1997 the Mexican government spent US$7 billion on roads,

Guerrilla rebels meet in the southern state of Guerrero, site of a 1990s uprising.

schools, hospitals, and drinking water systems in Chiapas, but the quality of life for most of the Indians in the mountains has still not improved.

Mexicans took the Chiapas problem to heart. Countless newspaper articles for and against the rebels, and public demonstrations in support of and critical of the ELZN appeared more and more frequently as the uprising continued. "Chiapas has awakened a social conscience that was asleep because we did not see the possibility of change," wrote Fernanda Navarro, a philosophy professor at the Nicolaita University in Morelia.

As political analyst Jesús Silva-Herzog commented in the Mexico City newspaper *Reforma,* in 1997 Mexico took "two paths, votes and bullets." Mexico is finally changing, but it remains to be seen if change will come peacefully through the polls or through the Mexican way of the past, violent insurrection.

ENVIRONMENTAL ISSUES

Though having a plot of land to farm and enough food to feed one's family are still the primary goals of a significant portion of Mexico's population, a growing number of Mexicans are becoming concerned about the deterioration in the country's environment. Among the nations of the world, Mexico ranks third in biodiversity, a measure of the total number of species of animals and plants found within the country's borders. For this reason alone, preservation of Mexico's natural environment is important to everyone.

Although the country faces serious environmental threats, Mexico's per capita contribution to air and water pollution, toxic emissions, depletion of natural resources, and the greenhouse effect are far below that of more industrialized areas of North America, Europe, and Asia. Outside the large cities and the maquiladora centers, the major threats to Mexico's environment come from illegal logging in old-growth tropical forests, overfishing in coastal waters, removal of slow-growing key plant species like ironwood for charcoal making, and overuse of pesticides.

Mexico seems, however, to be striving to catch up with the world's worst polluters. The number of factories and vehicles in Mexico is increasing rapidly. Mexico City has some of the worst air pollution in the world. Several maquiladora areas have been sites of severe toxic pollution.

The Mexican government is aware of the growing environmental problems and the Mexican people are becoming more concerned. Starting in 1988, Mexico began strengthening its environmental laws, although there was not often sufficient enforcement to put teeth into the laws. More recently Mexico began to set up biosphere reserves, an arrangement that theoretically balances human uses with protection of sensitive environmental areas. A biosphere reserve typically consists of a fully protected core zone surrounded by monitored limited-use areas where human activities will not disturb the protected sector. Examples of Mexico's twelve reserves are the Upper Sea of Cortés Biosphere Reserve (established in 1994) and the Calkmul Biosphere Reserve on the Yucatán Peninsula (established in 1989).

After numerous instances of toxic pollution traced to maquiladoras, many international and Mexican environmentalist groups complained that the maquilas were being used by foreigners to conduct pollution-causing business that would be prohibited back home. Because of these

 ## CHARCOAL MAKING

More than 250 privately owned charcoal pits smolder in Mexico, an enterprise that satisfies the U.S. market's hunger for steaks and burgers grilled over fragrant hardwood charcoal. Charcoal makers have found that ironwood trees work as well as mesquite, so thousands of ironwood trees have been cut down in the northern Mexican reaches of the Sonoran Desert.

In a 1994 *National Geographic* article, Tucson ethnobiologist Gary Nabhan calls ironwood "the keystone species of the Sonoran desert." The ironwood acts like a "nurse tree" for the fragile slow-growing saguaro cactus and other desert species. The Mexican government has enacted a law that forbids harvesting live ironwood, but in the remote regions of the desert it is a hard law to enforce.

Beginning in 1992, the International Sonoran Desert Alliance, with delegates from Mexican, Indian, and American cultures, has been working on strategies for protecting the natural and economic resources of the region. Meanwhile, as the U.S. market for hardwood charcoal continues to grow, mesquite and ironwood are getting harder to find in many areas.

The San Antonio River flows through the Montes Azules Biosphere Reserve in Selva Lacandona, Chiapas. The Mexican government established twelve reserves in an effort to restrict human encroachment on sensitive environmental areas.

well-publicized objections, Mexico and the United States focused their attention on the problem resulting in the most comprehensive environmental cleanup program in the history of either country.

MEXICO'S RELATIONSHIP WITH ITS NEIGHBOR TO THE NORTH

The relationship between Mexico and the United States is important and complex. Historical factors have often been an obstacle to better relations, but both countries now share a desire for a mutually beneficial relationship.

In addition to the historical factors, the Mexico-U.S. relationship is complicated by cultural and economic differences. On the other hand, interdependent economic interests, shared problems like the drug trade, and growing cooperation based on NAFTA are helping to shape a positive and constructive approach to the way the two countries deal with each other.

Mexican-U.S relations go far beyond diplomatic and official contacts to include extensive business, cultural, and educational ties. Along the border, state and local governments on both sides interact closely. The two countries

AMERICANS CROSSING THE BORDER INTO MEXICO

Stories about the problems surrounding illegal border crossers sneaking into the United States from Mexico appear in the news all the time. But it is not these people, mostly poor peasants who are desperately looking for work and a better life, who make the long border between Mexico and the United States the busiest international border in the world. Many Mexicans cross the border legally to work, shop, visit relatives, or be tourists. But many more North Americans cross the border to visit Mexico.

People from the United States visit Mexico for many reasons. They go to Mexico to study. The medical school in Guadalajara, for example, has a large number of students from the United States. Led by Cuernavaca south of Mexico City, several cities in Mexico have developed a minor industry in teaching Spanish language "immersion" courses that cater to students from the United States, Europe, and Asia.

North Americans cross the border to save money on dental work, cosmetic surgery, and pharmaceuticals. Some choose to live in Mexico near the border and cross back into the United States each day to work. Others retire in Mexico.

But the most common reason Americans travel to Mexico is for tourism. With its attractive blend of friendly people, ancient cultures, good food and drink, gorgeous beaches, and dramatic mountains, Mexico is the most-visited foreign destination of Americans.

Vehicles enter Mexico through the busy international border at Tijuana.

now cooperate in many areas, including trade, finance, law enforcement, immigration, agriculture, environment, fisheries, science, technology, and tourism. The U.S.-Mexico Binational Commission, formed in 1981, is the formal meeting point where the two governments work together to develop all these areas of mutual interest.

MEXICO'S GOVERNMENT

The full name of Mexico is the United Mexican States (known as *Estados Unidos Mexicanos*) since 1917. Officially described as a democratic federal republic, Mexico consists of thirty-one states and a Federal District (similar to Washington, D.C., in the United States).

Government powers are constitutionally divided between executive, legislative, and judicial branches. In practice, however, since the Revolution of 1910 much of the control of the country has been in the hands of the chief executive, the president of the republic. The president has the power to appoint the attorney general, cabinet members, supreme court justices, and top military leaders. There is no vice president.

The legislative branch, the congress, consists of a senate with 128 members (four from each state and the federal district) and a chamber of deputies with one representative for every 250,000 people.

The judicial system is headed by the supreme court of justice. There are twenty-one circuit courts and sixty-eight district courts. Judges are appointed for life.

In accordance with the Mexican Constitution of 1917, the president and the senators serve six-year terms and the deputies serve three-year terms. The senators and deputies cannot be reelected for the immediately succeeding term, and the president cannot be reelected at all. Personal freedoms, civil liberties, and suffrage for everyone over eighteen years of age are guaranteed.

Despite such democratic guarantees, twentieth-century Mexican politics have been notorious for election fraud. Recent efforts to reform election practices may be succeeding because for the first time since Mexico adopted the republican system in 1917, voters are electing representatives other than those endorsed by the ruling party.

Though Mexico's federal government is a democracy with elections at least theoretically contested by multiple parties, in practice the Institutional Revolutionary Party (PRI) wielded absolute one-party control for most of the twentieth century. For example, the PRI won thirteen consecutive presidential elections. Beginning in the 1990s, however, a new wave of change swept the country as other parties, especially the National Action Party (PAN) and the Democratic Revolution Party (PRD), began to erode the PRI monopoly. Now several states and a number of big cities (including Mexico City) have non-PRI governors and mayors.

For the first time in several generations, post-1997 Mexico has a multiparty, democratic government to set the country's course. The PRI still holds the lion's share of power in the country but it is no longer without strong opposition. Besides the disgraced PRI, Mexican political parties include *Partido Accion Nacional* (PAN), embraced by many Catholics; *Partido de la Revolución Democrática* (PRD), founded by Cuauhtémoc Cárdenas; *Partido Verde Ecologista de Mexico* (PVE), which is Mexico's pro-environment Green Party; and *Partido del Trabajo* (PT), which is the socialist-oriented workers' party.

RECONCILING MEXICO'S PAST ENTANGLES ITS PRESENT

The Palace of St. Lazarus in Mexico City is where the country's congress meets to decide on new legislation. There on the marble wall behind the imposing presidium is an emotional reminder of the difficulty of governing a country with such a complicated past.

On that wall are etched in gold letters the names of national heroes. On one column is the name of the man who is probably the most revered of Mexico's revolutionary leaders, Emiliano Zapata. On another column is Venustiano Carranza, the man who united Mexico after the revolution, and who is believed to have ordered Zapata's death.

In Mexico, history is so intricate that it is often difficult to tell the heroes from the villains. Even though dealing with the past will never be easy in Mexico, the country has successfully struggled through painful transitions before. Now the Mexican people, the people who survived the Spanish conquest, numerous invasions, many economic crises, several dictators, and recurrent natural disasters, must apply their resilience and resourcefulness to the problems of excessive population growth, urban crime, local revolts, environmental hazards, and economic crises that beset the nation today.

FACTS ABOUT MEXICO

GOVERNMENT

Full name of the country: *Estados Unidos Mexicanos*

Type: A federal republic headed by a president

Independence from Spain: September 16, 1810

National flag: Three vertical stripes of green, white, and red with the central white stripe showing the coat of arms, which depicts an eagle on a cactus holding a snake

National anthem: *Mexicanos, al grito de guerra* (Mexicans, when you hear the war cry)

NATIONAL HOLIDAYS

January 1	New Year's Day
February 5	Constitution Day
March 21	Birth of Benito Juárez
May 1	Labor Day
May 5	Anniversary of the Battle of Puebla
September 16	Independence Day
October 12	*Dia de la Raza*
November 2	Day of the Dead
November 20	Anniversary of the Mexican Revolution
December 12	Feast of Our Lady of Guadalupe
December 25	Christmas

PEOPLE

Total population (1996): 92.2 million

Population growth rate: 1.8 percent per year

Population doubling time: 26 years

Rural-urban distribution: 30 percent rural, 70 percent urban

Overall population density: about 110 people per square mile (43 per square km)

Life expectancy at birth: female, 72.3 years; male, 65.9 years

Major cities: Mexico City and the surrounding area of the Central Plateau is home to an estimated thirty million people. Other cities with over a million people are Guadalajara, Monterrey, Puebla, Leon, Ciudad Juárez, Culiacán, Mexicali, and Tijuana.

111

Religion: The vast majority (92 percent) is Roman Catholic, but there is no official religion. Preconquest Indian religion is combined with Catholicism in many places, and a small percentage of the population is Protestant, Jewish, Mormon, or Mennonite.

Languages: Spanish is the official language. Various Indian dialects, most related to Nahuatl and Mayan, are also spoken by many Indians.

Work week: Averages 45 hours

Education: Percent of population age 25 and over having: no primary education, 18 percent; some primary education, 34 percent; completed primary, 25 percent; some secondary, 14 percent; some postsecondary, 9 percent

Literacy: Total population over age 15: 95 percent literate

GEOGRAPHY

Area: 756,000 square miles (1,958,000 square km), eighth largest in the world, third largest in Latin America

Highest point: Pico de Orizaba (Citlaltépetl), 18,701 feet (5,700 meters)

Lowest region: The Yucatán, which varies from sea level to about 500 feet (152 meters) above sea level

Coastline: Over 6,000 miles (10,000 km) on the Pacific Ocean, Gulf of California (Sea of Cortés), Gulf of Mexico/Gulf of Campeche, and Caribbean Sea

Major rivers: The longest river is the Rio Bravo (Rio Grande in the United States). Other important river systems are the Rio Balsas (drains the southern portion of the Central Plateau) and the Grijalva-Usumacinta River (drains the Chiapas Highlands).

Mountains: Mountains cover two-thirds of Mexico.

Lakes: The largest lake is Lake Chapala in the state of Jalisco. It is 53 miles (86 km) long and 16 miles (25 km) wide.

CLIMATE

	July		January	
	C	F	C	F
La Paz	29	85	19	64
Monterrey	27	81	14	58
Guadalajara	21	69	15	59
Mexico City	16	61	13	55
Salina Cruz (south)	30	86	27	81
Merida	28	83	22	72

Annual rainfall: Most of the northern part of the country has less than 20 inches (50 cm); the Central Plateau has 20–39 inches (50–100 cm); the central coasts and most of the Yucatán have 39–79 inches (100–200 cm); and the southeastern coast has over 79 inches (200 cm).

ECONOMY

All monetary figures are in U.S. dollars—exchange rate in 1998 was approximately 8 pesos to the dollar.

Gross Domestic Product: $380 billion. Farming, fishing, and forestry contribute 7 percent of the GDP, industry 38 percent, and services 55 percent.

Annual per capita income: Approximately $4,000

Unemployment rate: Between 11 and 20 percent

Exports: Approximately $75 billion per year ($51 billion to the United States). Main exports are petroleum and petroleum products, silver, copper, zinc, sulfur, salt, coffee, cotton, fruits, vegetables, shrimp, computer and electrical components.

Imports: Approximately $80 billion per year (approximately $60 billion from the United States). Main imports are food products, transportation equipment, metalwork machinery, electrical equipment.

Major trading partners: The United States and Mexico are each other's largest trading partners. Europe, Japan, and Latin America are ranked next as Mexican export markets

ARMED FORCES

In 1995 Mexico had approximately 175,000 men and women on active military duty. That number, almost 50 percent higher than ten years earlier, makes Mexico's armed forces the thirtieth largest in the world. (Not only do the obvious world powers have larger military forces, but so do Israel, Cuba, Morocco, and Japan.)

Three-quarters of Mexico's military personnel are in the army with the remainder in the navy (*armada*) and the air force. All of the top officers are appointed by the president.

Mexico also has a national police force numbering about thirty thousand.

CHRONOLOGY

ca. 900–1519
Postclassic civilizations

ca. 1200
Aztecs first appear in central Mexico

1428
Aztecs take control of the Valley of Mexico

ca. 1500
Aztecs control all the lands and people of central Mexico

Popol Vuh (Mayan Book of the People) written

1517
First Spanish landing on present-day Mexico at Yucatán

1519
Cortés lands on Mexico's Gulf Coast and founds Veracruz

Montezuma killed, Cortés driven out of Tenochtitlán

1519–1821
Colonial period, pure-blood Spanish-born govern New Spain

1521
Cortés lays siege to Tenochtitlán

Cortés conquers Tenochtitlán

1524
Cortés hangs Cuauhtemoc, last ruler of the Aztecs

1537
Pope orders Spanish to stop enslaving the New World Indians

1540
First of the big silver discoveries, in Zacatecas

1804
Spanish king orders the church in the New World to turn over funds to him

1810
Hidalgo issues his *Grito de Dolores*, which ignites the Mexican Revolution

1811
Hidalgo and Allende crushed by the troops of the Spanish viceroy

1813
Morelos convenes the Chilpancingo Congress, armed rebellion resumes

1815
Morelos shot by firing squad

1821
Guerrero and Iturbide issue the *Plan de Iguala*

Treaty of Cordoba officially establishes New Spain's independence

1824
New constitution and adoption of the modern name of the country

1833
General Santa Anna seizes power for the first time and revokes the Constitution of 1824

1835
Santa Anna defeats the renegade Texans at the Alamo

1836
The Texans defeat Santa Anna and force him to grant them independence (Velasco Agreement)

1845
Mexico declares war on the United States when Texas joins the union

1847
U.S. forces capture Mexico City

1848
Treaty of Guadalupe Hidalgo ends Mexican-American War, giving lands to United States

1854
Santa Anna sells more land to the United States as the Gadsden Purchase

Santa Anna ousted for the last time

Juárez starts *La Reforma*

1857
La Reforma leads to new constitution

1858
Conservatives start a civil war, capture Mexico City,
throw out Constitution of 1857

1861
Liberals oust conservatives, Juárez elected president,
Constitution of 1857 reinstalled

1862
With encouragement from the conservatives,
Napoleon III's French forces invade Mexico

Mexicans defeat French in Battle of Puebla

1863
French counterattack, capture Mexico City, take over the
government of Mexico

1864
Napoleon III installs Maximilian as Emperor of Mexico

1867
French withdraw, Maximilian shot by firing squad, Juárez
elected president again

1871
Juárez becomes president for a fourth time, Díaz rebels
but quickly defeated

1872
Juárez dies from a heart attack

1876
Díaz becomes president and eventually dictator of Mexico

1910
Madero challenges Díaz, Díaz arrests him until after
the election

Madero calls for a general insurrection beginning the
Mexican Revolution

1911
Zapata joins Madero, Villa, Orozco, and other revolutionaries to attack Díaz

Díaz resigns

Madero elected president

1911 (continued)
Zapata rebuffed by Madero, joins with Villa and attacks
(*Tierra y Libertad*)

1913
Huerta arrests Madero, Madero killed, Huerta becomes
president

1913–1916
Zapata, Villa, Obregón, and Carranza, backed by United
States, attack Huerta

1916
Huerta flees as Obregón's forces enter Mexico City,
Carranza becomes president

Villa attacks train in United States, eludes pursuit by
General Pershing

1917
Carranza sponsors new constitution

1919
Zapata ambushed and killed by Carranza's soldiers

1920
Carranza assassinated

1921
Obregón elected president and begins Mexico's modern era

1923
Villa killed during a raid into the United States

1928
Obregón assassinated by a religious fanatic

Calles forms the PNR which became the PRI

1934
Cárdenas elected president

1938
Cárdenas nationalizes the petroleum industry

1942–1945
Mexico joins the Allies in World War II

1953
Women given the vote

1968

Troops under orders from President Díaz Ordaz fire on student protesters, killing many

First-ever Olympics in a Spanish-speaking country at Mexico City

1970

Voting age lowered to eighteen

1976

Huge oil reserves discovered in the south of the country

1982

World oil glut drives oil prices down

1985

Devastating earthquake hits Mexico City

1988

Corruption-plagued presidential elections put PRI candidate Salinas into office

1989

Cuauhtémoc Cárdenas, Salinas's opponent, starts the PRD party

1994

Chiapas rebellion starts led by ELZN

Salinas leaves office followed by a national economic crash and a trail of corruption

PRI candidate Zedillo elected to the presidency

1997

Cárdenas elected mayor of Mexico City, non-PRI candidates win in many elections

End of PRI domination of the Mexican congress

Suggestions for Further Reading

Louis B. Casagrande and Sylvia A. Johnson, *Focus on Mexico.* Minneapolis: Lerner, 1986. This book looks at Mexico with an emphasis on the lives of several young Mexicans living in a variety of modern-day situations.

Joe Cummings and Chicki Mallan, *Mexico Handbook.* Chico, CA: Moon, 1996. This is an excellent source for specific information on cities and regions of Mexico for the traveler or the merely interested.

Americo Paredes (ed. and trans.), *Folktales of Mexico.* Chicago: University of Chicago Press, 1970. Lively tales populated by strange characters and ancient lore (much of it dating from before the Spanish conquest) fill the pages of this easy-to-read volume.

Phyllis Shalant, *Look What We've Brought You from Mexico.* New York: Julian Messner, 1992. A fun little book full of unusual details, games, legends, and food items from Mexico.

R. Conrad Stein, *Enchantment of the World—Mexico.* Chicago: Childrens Press, 1984. An easy-to-read, basic overview of the country.

Time-Life Books (ed.), *Mexico.* Amsterdam, Netherlands: Time-Life Books, 1985. A beautifully illustrated book that provides additional depth, especially in twentieth-century Mexican social and political issues.

WORKS CONSULTED

Anita Brenner, *The Wind That Swept Mexico: The History of the Mexican Revolution of 1910–1942.* Austin: University of Texas Press, 1971.

Alfonso Caso, *The Aztecs, People of the Sun.* Norman: University of Oklahoma Press, 1958.

Bernal Diaz del Castillo, *The Discovery and Conquest of Mexico.* New York: Grove Press, 1958.

William Langewiesche, *Cutting for Sign.* New York: Pantheon Books, 1993.

Michael Meyer and William Sherman, *The Course of Mexican History (5th ed.).* New York: Oxford University Press, 1995.

David Nevin, *The Mexican War.* Alexandria, VA: Time-Life Books, 1978.

Henry B. Parkes, *A History of Mexico.* Boston: Houghton Mifflin, 1960.

Octavio Paz, *The Labyrinth of Solitude: Life and Thought in Mexico.* Trans. Lysander Kemp. New York: Grove Press, 1961.

Peter Rosset with Shea Cunningham, "Understanding Chiapas." Internet: http://www.ezln.org

U.S. Bureau of the Census, *Detailed Statistics on the Urban and Rural Population of Mexico: 1950–2010.* Washington, DC: U.S. Bureau of the Census, 1992.

Priit Vesilind, "The Sonoran Desert," *National Geographic,* September 1994.

Thomas Weil, et al., *Area Handbook for Mexico.* Washington, DC: U.S. Government Printing Office, 1996.

INDEX

PICTURE CREDITS

ABOUT THE AUTHOR

William G. Goodwin lives in San Diego. He is a graduate of the University of California at Los Angeles and has also undertaken graduate study in biochemistry, education, and English. He is a writer and speaker specializing in youth, management, and industry. He has also taught high school sciences, owned and operated a sailing school, written scripts for educational videos, and built a forty-three-foot sailboat. Mr. Goodwin has lived in Mexico, Brazil, and Asia. He has two teenagers, Gideon and Marilyn, and a very friendly bird named Pepper.